THE COMPLETE
HOW TO KAZOO

BARBARA STEWART

WORKMAN PUBLISHING / NEW YORK

Published simultaneously in Canada
by Thomas Allen & Son Limited

Library of Congress Cataloging-in-Publication
Data is available.

ISBN-13: 978-0-7611-4221-8
ISBN-10: 0-7611-4221-5

Workman Publishing Company, Inc.
708 Broadway
New York, NY 10003-9555
www.workman.com

Printed in Mexico

First printing July 2006

10 9 8 7 6 5 4 3 2 1

To Kazoodaphiles everywhere

"If nobody wants to go to your concert,
nothing will stop them."—Isaac Stern

Acknowledgments

I gratefully acknowledge the enthusiastic assistance of Kazoodaphiles who contributed blood, sweat, essential material—and a lot of notes over the years, especially Lance & Lisa Lehmberg; Chuck Morey, ML & David Perlman (inventor Macaroni Kaminsky); photographer John Menihan Jr; Dr. Ruth Abrahams; my daughter Whitney Stewart (without whom this book would not have been possible) and my older brother (without whom this book would not have been necessary). Editors Omninsky Kaminsky & Suzanne Rafer; Kazoophonists everywhere (including but not limited to Lance, Lisa, Chuck, Franco Spoto, Diana Benton, Jim Walker, Alan Bunin, Herb Wise, Mark Wolf, Simon Pontin, Ruth Cahn, Marguerite Hickey, June Forster, Jerry LaMarsh, Dave Amelee, Rob Goodling, et al.); my daughter Allison; nephew Jeff Dean at Google; Major Carl R. Fehrenbacher MAJ, GS, RD PAO, ACoS G3, USASETAF (ABN); James Bradley 173d Airborne; and NY Army National Guard, Rochester. Yale Drama School & Columbia professors Howard Stein, Gerald Schoenfeld, Ming Cho Lee, William Warfel and Jane Greenwood; the late Tony

Randall & Heather, Martin Sheen, Patrick Tull, Michael York, Lynn Redgrave & Georgianne Walken (National Actors Theatre/Broadway). Norman at The Ritz; Claire Oesch & Victor at Café Des Artistes; Michael at O'Neal's; Mike Ditka; Peter Coy. North Country contributors Ross & Janie Reynolds; Liz Braun-DeMarco; historian Grace Good, Jeff Neiman (Universal) & recording engineer David Greene (with 3 e's). Also Helga & Paul Morgan; Hank & Ann Couch; Ben Bisbee; Dr. Bruce Corsello; Kate Driesen & Dave Fogg; Mary & Jim Spindler; physicist Michael Eibl, Bayer Company, Germany; Professor Masako Toribara (Eastman School); Maestros David Gilbert, Nancia D'Alimonte, Jerrold Morgulas & David Zinman; opera satirist Anna Russell; actor Paul Newman; Peter Schickele; Garrison Keillor; Houston Allred; Kazooperman (Rob Spoor); Mark, Eric & all at Genesistems; Maurice Van de Laar (Dutch connection); costume designer Paul Spadone; John Margulis; Gideon Schein; Wally (Famous) Amos; Pamela Massey (ASCAP Kazoo Dept); Louise Jones (NYC Yale Club Librarian); Dr. David Evans (Memphis State); Robert Sheldon (Smithsonian & Library of Congress); Indiana Music Library; Eastman Music Library; Rochester Public Library; Artist Ronald Searle; Nonnie Locke; Dan Brock; John Elberfeld; John Goldman; Jeff Newman; Amtrak crews; Dr. Herb & Suzanne Golomb; Van Bortle Subaru; David & Sue Callan-Harris; Vincent, Brielle & Annamarie Salvatico; Heather Carroll; Conti family (Tracy, JB, Olivia & Michael); Orri Antonsson & Greta Antonsdottir;

v

St. John Fisher students; Jeff Hsu at Technoland; Mishka the Master Builder (Peter), Sally, Jason & staff at Staples; Lucy LoPresiti at Karen's Crafts; Gemma at Crafts & Pieces; Colonial Belle; Fairport Football (Spiderman, Batman & Robin); Fairport Highway Dept; America's patriots who protect our creative freedom; ancestor David Bushnell (submarine inventor, but not responsible for cigar shape of kazoos); Counting Sheep from Serta Mattress; The Aflac Duck; Sir Arthur Shafman; and Lynn Johnston, faithful literary agent. Finally, I am grateful to Steve Jobs, who gave me a Macintosh computer in 1984, which allowed me to delete almost as fast as I could type, creating text of workable size for publication. (I also use PCs, but Bill Gates has never sent me anything.)

Contents

Keep America Humming viii

CHAPTER ONE: **Kazoo Roots** 1

CHAPTER TWO: **Your Instrument** 15

CHAPTER THREE: **Rudiments** 35

CHAPTER FOUR: **Ensemble Kazooing** 87

CHAPTER FIVE: **Everyday** (and Special-Occasion) **Kazooing** 153

Appendix 187

Keep America Humming

If you can hum, sing, or talk, you can successfully kazoo. At this very moment, millions of satisfied kazooists all over the globe are delighting in the kazoo's distinctive sounds. Yet, sadly, the kazoo continues to be an object of derision and scorn among those ignorant of its extraordinary qualities. The time has come to set the record straight and allow the kazoo to take its rightful place in the world of music.

For the uninitiated, the kazoo is a small cigar-shape plastic or metal instrument that produces a pleasant buzzing when the player hums, sings, or speaks into it. The instrument itself has no musical capabilities, so everything depends on the kazooist. In fact, it has been said that the instrument may actually be a hindrance to the kazooist, that "the kazoo is to music what the full-body cast is to ballet." But this is a very shortsighted view. The kazoo's total dependency on the kazooist is precisely what makes kazooing a uniquely individual musical expression.

Most important, the kazoo is a musical instrument, not simply a toy. Thus, for all kazooists, the fundamental rule of musicianship applies: "Practice, practice, practice . . . but not near the neighbors."

The Kazoo and Its Place in the Musicological Hierarchy

Musicologists are great experts on many things, but the kazoo is not one of them. Preoccupied with other matters, musicologists have tended to classify anything that buzzes as a kazoo. The kazoo, eunuch flute, mirliton, Hum-a-zoo, zobo, and other, similar instruments have all been wantonly and erroneously thrown together and their names used interchangeably. Some have even gone so far afield as to confuse the kazoo with the ocarina (sweet potato) and such items as the Jew's harp, the harmonica, or the whoopee cushion. (Fortunately, most of these experts remain cloistered in academia and do not frequent the out-of-doors. Otherwise, the confusion might extend to include chain saws, model airplanes, and even killer bees.) Kazoos are like toothbrushes: Anyone can use one, everyone needs one, but you rarely see anyone writing about toothbrushes except dentists.

The kazoo is actually a member of the musical classification "membranophone." This category consists of percussion instruments that produce sound through the use of a stretched membrane. Further, it is part of the subcategory "mirliton," a group of instruments that disguises or modifies sounds produced vocally (or by another instrument) through the medium of vibrating membranes. The membrane causes the sound to be amplified and distorted, giving a nasal buzzing quality.

There are a thousand varieties of mirlitons throughout the world. They share the same principle of sound production but exist in varying sizes, shapes, and permutations in different countries. This vastly popular group of instruments may be further subcategorized as either free mirlitons (such as the comb and tissue paper or the turkey call) or tube or vessel mirlitons (such as the zobo, kazoo, and eunuch flute).

Just as more conventional instruments have specific names, so do the types of tube mirlitons. "Violin," for example, is a specific name for a particular shape and type of chordophone, subcategory

Hum's the word.

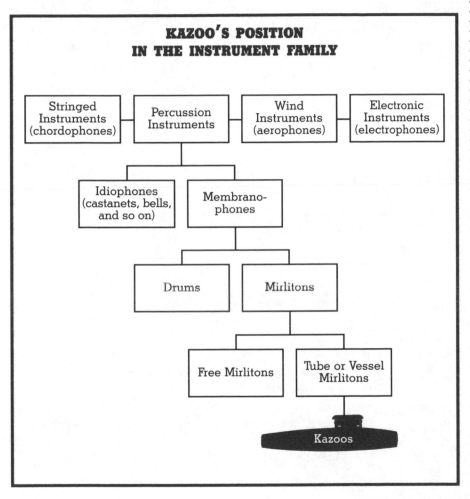

**KAZOO'S POSITION
IN THE INSTRUMENT FAMILY**

Stringed Instruments (chordophones) — Percussion Instruments — Wind Instruments (aerophones) — Electronic Instruments (electrophones)

Percussion Instruments:
- Idiophones (castanets, bells, and so on)
- Membranophones

Membranophones:
- Drums
- Mirlitons

Mirlitons:
- Free Mirlitons
- Tube or Vessel Mirlitons

Tube or Vessel Mirlitons:
- Kazoos

lute. No sensible person would refer to a violin as a "lute," although it does belong to this group of instruments. Nor would we use "violin" as a synonym for the hurdy-gurdy or bass viol, even though they are related in principles of sound production. In like fashion, we correctly use "kazoo" to refer to a specific instrument, the American version of a tube mirliton.

kazoo (ka-zoo') *n.* 1. A manufactured version of an Afro-American folk instrument, U.S. in origin. An auxiliary instrument of the membranophone category, a specific type of tube mirliton, in which sound is vocally produced by humming, singing, or speaking into the larger end of an open-ended, cigar-shape tube. A stretched membrane in the top of the instrument is set in vibration by the voice-activated air column, which modifies the sound to produce a nasal buzzing timbre. The tube is usually made of metal or plastic, with a removable turret on top that unscrews or lifts out to allow replacement of the resonating membrane. The kazoo is closely related to but not identical to the abeng, akasitori, bazoo, Bigotphone (Bigophone), cantophone, Düderli, eggwara, eunuch flute, faggotzug, fipple flute, Flatsche, flauto di voce, free mirliton (comb and tissue paper), French mirliton, hewgag, Huma-zoo, konene, mbanakum, megablaster, merlotina, nyastaranga, onion flute, shalmei, Skalmej, Strählorgelj, sudrophone, turkey caller, varinette, vocaphone, zazah, and zobo.

CHAPTER ONE

KAZOO ROOTS

An African Link

What a culture considers sacred is often obscured in veils of secrecy that conceal its true purpose. Such is the case with the African mirlitons, related instruments, but not identical to kazoos (which were an American invention). While mirlitons were known to be used in sacred ceremonies, until recently the exact purpose of the instrument remained largely a mystery to the outside world.

Most musicologists and anthropologists assumed African mirlitons were used for producing musical sounds, but this is not so. African mirlitons were primarily used as voice disguisers and as weapons of intimidation, not as musical instruments.

Mirlitons appeared in a surprising number of cultures throughout Africa. They varied considerably in size and shape from tribe to tribe, yet a style found in many cultures is a hollow tube, covered at each end by a membrane, with a center mouthpiece. Tubes are made of an endless variety of materials, including bones, reeds, gourds, corn stalks, buffalo horns, and even parts of human bone.

In Africa, mirlitons were used to impersonate the voices of the dead, to make terrifying sounds and bring messages from the spirit world. The male ceremonial figure concealed his true identity by enshrouding himself in robes (and often a mask), using a mirliton to disguise his voice. He communicated the messages from the "spirits of the dead" in this manner, and the distorted sounds were interpreted by tribal officials to make sure the meaning was clear.

The effectiveness of the intimidation depended on preserving the secret of the existence of voice disguisers (mirlitons), since once the source was revealed, fear of the unknown would no longer be a control mechanism. For this reason, to divulge the secret to an outsider, or to a woman or an uninitiated male tribe member, was an offense punishable by death.

Birth of the Kazoo in America

Since disclosing the secret of the tribal "voice disguiser" meant death, it seems unlikely that any African slaves would have held "mirliton show and tell" for their captors. However, it is plausible that an American descendant, generations removed from tribal ritual, was familiar with the mirliton, perhaps even without knowing its sacred function. Legend has it the kazoo was invented in Macon, Georgia, in the 1840s by Alabama Vest, an American black, and made to his specifications by Thaddeus Von Clegg, a German-American clockmaker. It was reported to

THE FIRST METAL KAZOO

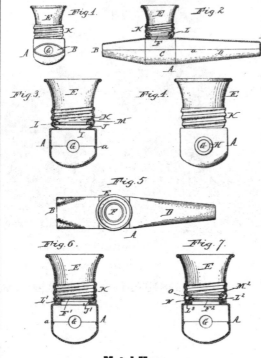

Metal Kazoo
Patented by George Dana Smith,
Buffalo, New York, 1902

In some earlier-model kazoos, the resonator was located at one side or across from the passage for breath. According to Smith's patent, side location from the escape hole created problems by confining air vibrations to internal resonation only. Cross location resulted in insufficient escape for voice waves and breath, making the instruments "practically valueless in the hands of an unskilled operator." The turret served as a collection device for resonated sound to assure success for virtually anyone.

AGAIN, THE FIRST METAL KAZOO (1902)

**Metal kazoo made in the first year of manufacturing
by The Kazoo Company, Inc., Buffalo, New York**

The package label reads "Play with trumpet lip. Do not blow, but hum, speak, laugh or make an imitation. Plays any tune, imitates any bird or animal, bagpipes, snare drum and Punch and Judy. Bands using it as a mouthpiece on brass instruments . . . produce excellent music without fingering keys. Used with astonishing results at society meetings, home, clubs, church choirs, entertainments, dances, serenades, picnics, outings, excursions, campaigns, bicycle and marching clubs, quartettes, choruses and shows. Turn trumpet slightly for tenor, baritone or soprano voices. Keep vibrator side of washer down."

have been exhibited at the Georgia State Fair in 1852 before being sold to a toy manufacturer, who produced it under the name "Down South Submarine."[1]

[1]Green, Parp, *Melody Maker and Rhythm,* October 20, 1951, page 11.

Although I have not found other reports to substantiate this particular account, the *Oxford English Dictionary* and *Grove's Dictionary of Music and Musicians* agree that the kazoo is American. And if we can't believe *Grove's Dictionary* and the *OED,* who *can* we trust?

Whatever its exact origins, the submarine-shape kazoo was an actual invention, an acoustic improvement on more primitive varieties of mirlitons, with the addition of a turret on top (not seen in African or other mirlitons), which acted as a collector for exterior vibrations. The turret's screw-on flange also allowed easy replacement of damaged or worn membranes.

The kazoo took on an important role as a musical instrument in early blues and country music in the United States. From the 1840s on, musicians used kazoos to amplify their voices, making them loud enough to be heard over banjos and other instruments. Later, the kazoo made an easy

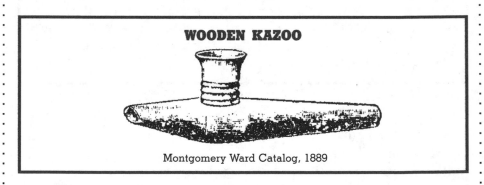

WOODEN KAZOO

Montgomery Ward Catalog, 1889

transition to jazz, and along with the comb and tissue paper, it would appear throughout jazz history. The kazoo was inexpensive and readily available, and in the hands of an expert, phenomenal effects could be achieved.

Although the American kazoo was not intended primarily as a weapon, some critics argue that an element of intimidation remains. Particularly convincing on this point are school bus drivers intimidated by exuberant kazoo-wielding children.

Overseas Invasions and Alliances

The American kazoo was largely unknown in the United Kingdom before the Great War (1917). However, research specialist Rudolph A. Clemen Jr., of the American Red Cross Library, noted that

Physicist Albert Einstein, the genius who discovered the theory of relativity, was known to have played the violin, musical spoons, and the kazoo—but not necessarily simultaneously.

kazoos were undoubtedly part of shipments to American servicemen from World War I on. Documentation indicates that from 1917 to 1919, "8 pianos and 463 other musical instruments were shipped to the British Isles and distributed free to American soldiers and sailors." Small instruments were also included in Red Cross boxes sent to servicemen in England and France. Mr. Clemen agrees that although there are other possibilities, kazoos are most likely, due to the higher cost of harmonicas and the difficulty of fitting anything much larger into Red Cross boxes.

English Tommy Talker Bands of the 1920s and 1930s

There is little question that Yankee kazooists infected the British Isles with enthusiasm. According to an article in *Musical Traditions,*[2] the famous Tommy Talker Bands of the West Riding (Yorkshire, England) were humor-driven fun-time bands of the working classes. They came into

prominence after World War I, using simple, homemade music-makers and including kazoos as the main instrument (referred to as a "Tommy Talker," bazooka, gazooka, hooter, or submarine). They reportedly marched from village to village, collecting money and leading parades for festivals and carnivals.

Although there are no reports of Pied Pipers leading them astray, Tommy Talker bands

[2]Ronnie Wharton and Arthur Clarke, "The Tommy Talker Bands of the West Riding," article MT072 from *Musical Traditions* No. 1, mid-1983.

largely disappeared during World War II, amid lighthearted rumors that bands were simply too bombed to continue. If true, a resurgence seems inevitable.

Where Kazoos Come From

Modern corporate connections for kazoo manufacture and distribution are more complicated than would seem possible and more intricate to untangle than offshore investment resources buried in Swiss bank vaults. However, here is the information as I understand it. There appear to be only three major current kazoo manufacturing operations in America:

1. *Kazoobie Company* of Port Richie, Florida (www.kazoos.com), makes quality plastic kazoos, distributes metal and wooden models, and offers novelty products that include custom-imprinted kazoos, noisemakers and other fun instruments, chocolate kazoos, necklace lavalieres, books, recordings, etc. President Rick Hubbard, known as "The King of Kazoo," is a performing kazooist and leader of world-record kazoo bands.

2. The original metal *Kazoo Company, Inc.,* in Eden, New York, sold rights for their models (including band-instrument shapes) to Woodstock Percussion in 1997. They now make only limited numbers for museum

Two kazoos is company; three is a band.

demonstrations and sale in their gift shop.

3. *Heartwood Creations, Inc.,* located in Rockford, Illinois (www.heartwood.com), crafts a funky kazoo of cherry wood, which comes in a velvet carrying bag.

Other Kazoo Sources

Most kazoos are manufactured in China or Taiwan, and sold through American distributors

Trophy Music of Cleveland, Ohio, offers good-quality plastic models, along with submarine-shape metal kazoos, the Hum-a-Zoo, and a full line of associated toy instruments.

The Hohner Company of Richmond, Virginia, well known for its harmonicas, distributes a good-quality plastic kazoo.

Woodstock Percussion of Woodstock, New York, purchased the rights to original Eden Kazoo Company products— but does not produce band instrument–shape kazoos at this time. Woodstock distributes a metal kazoo (plug-in cap, not the original screw top) made in China, in addition to a plastic kazoo produced in Taiwan. Woodstock also distributes a full line of "toy instruments" and wind chimes to specialty toy and gift shops worldwide, including Cracker Barrel Country Stores.

Expensive (Elitist) Kazoos

L ike all other kazoos, high-end kazoos are, of course, self-limiting. However, for those who desire the perfect instrument for the "kazooist who has everything," keep in mind that no kazoo is greater than the sum of its kazooist.

Heartland Hummer

(Artisan's Kazoo)

Made of cherry wood by
Heartwood Creations in
Rockford, Ill., this is one of the
few remaining American kazoo
manufacturers. Hand-hewn,

quality superstructure $\frac{1}{2} \times 1\frac{1}{2} \times 4"$ in elegant velvet case. Kazoo

---

SAFETY CONSIDERATIONS

- Master the backing-up-truck beeping sound (high-pitched repetitions of "eep-eep," see page 84) to alert listeners when you plan to kazoo backward.

- Do not kazoo in the road unless it has been cleared of traffic as a parade route.
- Never kazoo in the direct path of elephant, buffalo, or other animal herds.

---

swings open laterally to allow replacement of the resonator, centrally located in the instrument's interior. To locate retail dealers, see www.heartwood.com or e-mail craftsales@heartwood.com.

Silver Kazoo

Custom ordered from Forsythe Jewelry (forsythe@rochester.rr.com), this stunning 3-inch sterling silver model designed by Lenore Roskow is an authentic "piccolo" kazoo. It is acoustically best suited to soprano voice and to the aesthetic taste and pocketbook of the elite. Additional

> **Kazoobie doobie doo!**

charge for monogram or silver chain for evening wear.

Gold-plated Kazoo

Known as the "Humdinger," it is made of metal plated with 24K gold. Plating does not perceptibly alter the tone quality, but it does raise the status and the retail price.

Newcastle Drum Kazoo Cousins

Modeled after more conventional brass instruments, these supersounding voice-activated instruments are designed along the lines of 19th-century quality zoboes. These are elite British versions among their American kazoo cousins and require a bit more skill to resonate the tonal center, but the results are extraordinary. Stainless steel structure is manufactured in Sheffield (England), where the original tableware for the *Titanic* was made. Available at www.newcastledrum.co.uk/steel.

Barbara Stewart Custom Kazoos™

Available online at the Kazoobie Kazoo site (www.kazoos.com), these products and accessories offer unique additions to your complete kazooing experience.

SECONDARY USES FOR A KAZOO

- To replace stolen hood ornaments on Rolls-Royces
- As a pestle for grinding corn
- To snuff out candles
- As a curling iron for on-the-go coiffing (metal only)
- For starting fires (use two wooden kazoos, a magnifying glass, and a Boy Scout)
- To baste a turkey

The Instant Music Kit, Joyful Noise Holiday Wreath, Stealth Kazoo, and Keep America Humming kazoos will be available as soon as I get around to it.

Buyer Beware

Although most companies are committed to quality control, there may be others that are not. Kazoos with removable turrets and resonators (small parts) are not recommended for children under the age of three. Sharp edges or unsafe paint are unacceptable for any age. Also watch out for resonators that have been punctured or that are permanently attached (soldered, painted, or glued) to the barrel, which renders the instrument useless.

CHAPTER TWO

YOUR INSTRUMENT

Choosing an Instrument

For those who bought this book, the choice has already been made. But, sooner or later, you may need or wish to purchase a new kazoo.

Your Student Model

The kazoo you received with this manual is the professional student model made of Amoco polyolefins-polypropylene homopolymer plastic. It is manufactured in America by Kazoobie, Inc. In my personal judgement, it has a:

• Specific gravity of 0.88–0.92

• Water absorption @ 24 hours of 0.0100%

• Melting point of 160°C (320°F)

• Flash point of 329°C or 675°F

• Molecular weight greater than 200,000 (without membrane)

Tod Seelie

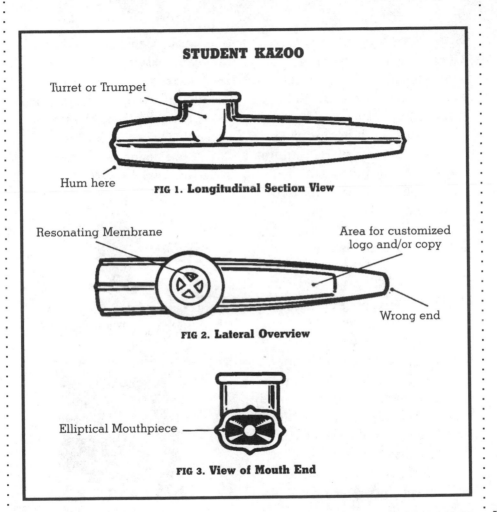

STUDENT KAZOO

Turret or Trumpet

Hum here

FIG 1. Longitudinal Section View

Resonating Membrane

Area for customized logo and/or copy

Wrong end

FIG 2. Lateral Overview

Elliptical Mouthpiece

FIG 3. View of Mouth End

King Kazoo (metal)

The basic metal kazoo is a submarine or cigar shape. It is constructed of tin sheet metal (which is sometimes gold plated) and painted with nontoxic paint.

At the top is a turret containing the resonating membrane, which is also called a vibrator, resonator, or diaphragm, but it is usually referred to by professional kazooists as "the little paper thing on the top." It is held in place in the turret by a plug-in flange or threaded spadger.

Metal kazoos are manufactured by a stamping procedure. The halves are punched from lithographed sheets of tin-plated steel, which are between 0.008 and 0.012 of an inch thick (the same material is used to make tin cans). The halves are then shaped with presses and rolled in quantity. Separate machines are used to stamp and mount the diaphragms (resonators). The placement of the membrane inside the turret and the turret assembly (screwing in the flange) are done manually by kazoo assembly workers.

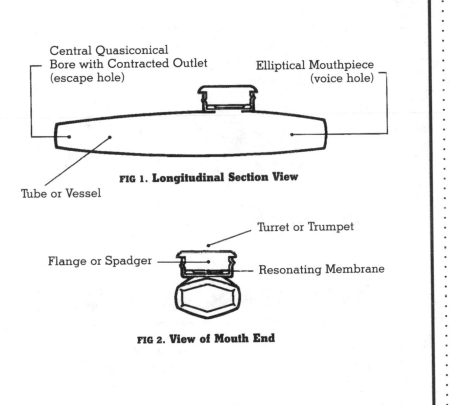

KING KAZOO

Central Quasiconical Bore with Contracted Outlet (escape hole)

Elliptical Mouthpiece (voice hole)

Tube or Vessel

FIG 1. Longitudinal Section View

Turret or Trumpet

Flange or Spadger

Resonating Membrane

FIG 2. View of Mouth End

Resonating Membranes

Until recently, the resonating membrane used in metal kazoos was made exclusively of animal membrane, stretched and held in place by a tiny circular frame of cardboard. This membrane, extracted from the stomachs of sheep or cows (without their consent), is the same material used to cap perfume bottles, since it is impervious to the scent and resists water and solvents.

Rising sheep prices in Australia and competition from dog food companies created a dramatic increase in the price of the membrane, causing many kazoo companies to go to a plastic (silicon) resonator in the 1970s. This new resonator was more durable and less susceptible to breakage but gave a slightly sharper and less pleasant tone color.

Resonators are now commonly made of polyurethane plastic, waxed paper, or glassine weighing paper (commonly used in pharmaceutical manufacturing operations or as dividing paper in boxed candy).

The least desirable resonators are waxed paper, often without a cardboard frame to stretch or anchor them. Their ability to repel moisture diminishes quickly, so they are quickly rendered nonfunctional. Contrary to folklore, tissue paper and, even worse, non-European toilet paper are unacceptable, since they lack sharp resolution or resonance. They also disintegrate on exposure to moisture.

Acoustical Properties of Kazoo Sound

The column of sound waves, supplied by the vocalization of the kazooist, travels into the barrel of the kazoo through the mouth hole. When sound waves strike the resonating membrane, they are magnified and distorted. In the interior of the resonating chamber (barrel, tube, or vessel), these vibrations are propelled in all directions, resonating from the membrane and meeting new vibrations as they are set in motion. The sounds escape primarily through the turret, although some are diverted to the anterior end (opposite the mouthpiece). The effect is a series of complicated layers of overtones, which the listener hears as a buzzing timbre (fuzzy pitch).

Exterior vibrations (outer-air vibrations) strike the top of the resonating membrane. Some ricochet back into the external air and some are entrapped in the turret, causing them to interact with new sets of vibrations.

The best kazoo sounds occur at the turret outlet. This is because vibrations there are denser and less airy sounding than the weaker inner voice vibrations that must travel long distances and have less interaction with the membrane.

In the case of stringed instruments, sympathetic vibrations occur when a string is set in motion in response to vibrations of the same pitch from another source. For example, a "ghost effect" can be achieved while standing next to a piano and playing a pitch on the violin. The piano string of the same

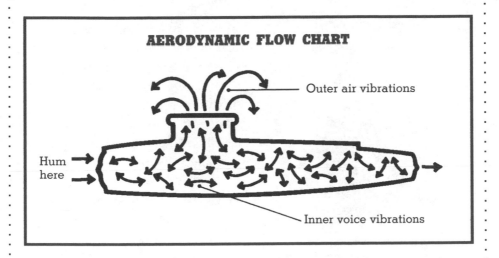

AERODYNAMIC FLOW CHART

Outer air vibrations

Hum here →

Inner voice vibrations

pitch frequency will begin to spontaneously vibrate, causing the eerie "ghost effect." Sympathetic vibration occurs only in response to vibrations of the same pitch.

On the other hand, the principle of kazoo sound production is what we shall term "antagonistic vibration." The resonating membrane, rather than being sympathetic to a particular pitch, is undiscriminating—it is capable of being set in motion by nearly anything. The sound of the voice, which sets the membrane in vibration, is rebounded in all directions from the membrane, setting up a conflict with any new vibrations being created by the player. This results in a bombardment of sound and produces the fuzzy nasal timbre so highly valued by the kazooist.

POST-KAZOO DISTRESS SYNDROME
To prevent post-kazoo distress, always keep an extra instrument on hand in case of loss or theft.

Care and Maintenance of the Kazoo

The kazoo should be cleaned as needed, since things such as dirt, spittle, dust, insects, and tar spots adhere firmly to the body and may damage the paintwork. (They also taste terrible.) Pipe cleaners or cotton swabs can be used to clear the tube of foreign matter. During the winter, special care should be taken to wash off all road salt residue as soon as possible to prevent corrosion of the metal kazoo.

Washing (plastic or metal models)
When washing the kazoo, do not expose it to direct sunlight. For plastic models, simply wipe the outer surfaces with a damp sponge or soft cloth. If the membrane is not removable, do not submerge the kazoo in water. For metal models, remove the membrane from the turret and set aside. Soften up the dirt on the inside of the kazoo with a water jet and then rinse the whole body with a light jet until the dirt has loosened. Wash off the dirt with a tiny sponge,

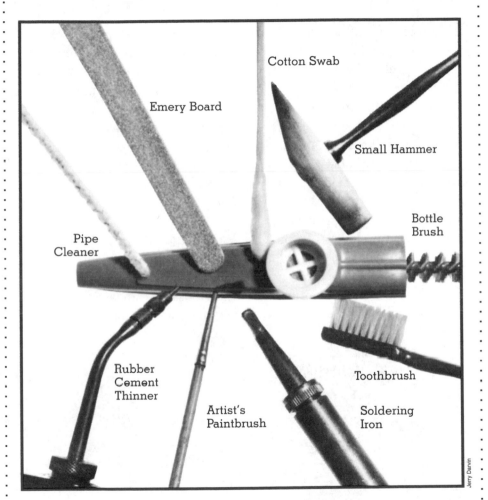

Cotton Swab

Emery Board

Small Hammer

Bottle Brush

Pipe Cleaner

Rubber Cement Thinner

Artist's Paintbrush

Toothbrush

Soldering Iron

Jerry Darvin

using plenty of lukewarm, not hot, water. Then dry carefully with a soft clean cloth. Place the membrane in the turret.

Note: Asphalt spots, tar pittings, and gum wads can be removed with kerosene or tar removers, but this may leave a bitter aftertaste, besides possibly being toxic. For this reason, kazooists experiencing severe maintenance problems of this nature are advised to discard the instrument and buy a new one.

In humid climates, watch for biological growth or base-side scum in the interior channel of the tube. A clear solution of household cleanser with ammonia will alleviate the biological growth problem but may be injurious to the player. In this case, it is also best to discard the offending instrument and replace it with a new, uncontaminated one.

Polishing
(metal kazoos only)

The kazoo does not need polishing unless the surface finish begins to lose its luster and

> **To err is human,
> to kazoo divine.**

against unfavorable weather. For the most part, waxing is not necessary until at least a year after delivery of the kazoo.

normal washing is no longer sufficient to make it shine again. Under normal conditions, it is sufficient to polish the kazoo once or twice a year, assuming that it is well cared for and washed as soon as it becomes dirty or clogged. Before the kazoo is polished, it should be carefully washed and dried to prevent scratches on the paintwork.

Use household paraffin (the same wax that is used to seal home-canned foods) or mustache wax to polish your kazoo. Before applying, be sure the surface is absolutely clean. Waxing should be considered neither a substitute for polishing nor a necessary protection for the paintwork

Body Work
(metal kazoos only)

To prevent the kazoo from sustaining dent damage, it is important as a preventive measure to caution all kazooists to watch where they step. Care should also be exercised to avoid dropping the instrument. If damaged, standard body-work techniques may be used to hammer out dents. Touch-up procedures should then be followed.

Paint Touch-up
(metal kazoos only)

Paint damage requires immediate attention to prevent rusting. Make it a habit to check the

finish regularly and touch it up if necessary, particularly in the mouthpiece area. Minor scratches and chips can be repaired by using nontoxic primer and paint. For deep scars:

1. Lightly scrape or sand the damaged surface to break the edges of the scar.

2. Thoroughly mix the primer and apply it with a small brush, toothpick, or matchstick.

3. When the primed surface is dry, the paint can be applied by brush. Mix paint thoroughly and apply several thin paint coats, letting surface dry after each application.

Use of Bore Oil (metal kazoos)

Instrumentalists often ask whether they should use bore oil on the kazoo to prevent sticking of the movable parts. I personally use it sparingly and only when the instrument is severely infested with bores.

Resonator Check
(plastic and metal kazoos)

At regular intervals, the resonating membrane should be checked for irregularities or

HAZARDS TO KAZOOING

- Rust (outdoor and underwater performances)
- Natural disasters such as tornados, electrical storms, and blizzards
- Unnatural disasters such as artistically unappreciative crowds
- Wrong turns into ravines, gravel pits, or swamp and bog areas
- Turret impedimenta (thumbs from rival bands, illegally parked gum)
- Muggers and marauding pirate bands
- Attacking dog packs
- Stampeding parade livestock, such as horses, ponies, and spitting llamas
- Long marches off short piers
- Vehicular instrument flatteners (steamrollers, trains, and band buses)
- Planes, pigeons, and other overhead bombers
- Potholes, bridgeouts, or sudden earthquake fissuring of the parade path

KAZOO SERVICE AND REPAIR CHART

CONDITION: KAZOO FAILS TO OPERATE

Possible Cause	Correction
1. Incorrect starting technique by operator	1. HUM . . . DO NOT BLOW! Repeat the word "doo" again and again into the larger end of the instrument to elicit response.
2. Defective vibrator	2. *For metal kazoos:* Unscrew or unplug turret, remove old vibrator. Replace with new unit. *For plastic kazoos:* Toss instrument and replace with one that works.
3. Diaphragm in upside down (metal only)	3. Remove turret, check diaphragm, making sure smooth side is down in the annulus. Side with raised cardboard edge must face up toward the turret.
4. Operator has thumb or fingers over end hole	4. Uncover the end. Try playing with no hands.

CONDITION: KAZOO FAILS TO OPERATE

Possible Cause	Correction
5. Operator has finger on vibrator	5. Remove finger (or thumb) from turret.
6. Dented body	6. Check for dents on body and turret. Call your insurance adjuster. Take to body shop for estimate before ordering repairs.
7. Broken hummer	7. Replace kazooist.

CONDITION: ERRATIC IDLE (MISFIRE)

Possible Cause	Correction
1. Gas (belching)	1. Try an antacid.
2. Hiccoughs	2. Place paper grocery bag on head. Breathe in and out.
3. Wrong place in music (for group kazooists)	3. Sit out until the next piece.

breaks. A hole in the membrane indicates an emergency situation, requiring immediate replacement. For any models with non-removable membranes, it means the purchase of an entire new instrument.

Rust Prevention and Degreasing (metal kazoo)

Your kazoo may have been treated against rust at its factory inspection. If so, only a touchup of the antirust treatment needs to be done. If touching up is necessary, this should be done immediately to prevent moisture from seeping in and consequently causing damage. While working

> **Kazoo happily and the world kazoos with you; weep and you'll rust alone.**

OTHER CONCERT USES FOR WD-40:

- Untangles kazoo lavalieres
- Removes spaghetti stains from clothing
- Gives playground slides a super-fast slide
- Lubricates wheel sprockets on tricycles, bicycles, and kazoomobiles (prop vans)
- Removes all traces of duct tape
- Cleans and removes bugs from turret screening mechanisms

---

on the body, remember to remove the membrane to prevent moisture damage.

It is said that Metal Kazoo Roadies need only two tools: WD-40 solvent and duct tape. WD-40 is for something that is supposed to move but doesn't;

duct tape for something that moves but isn't supposed to.

The most effective rust preventive solvent and degreaser for the kazoo flange and turret area is the WD-40 product, the "official multi-purpose problem-solver of NASCAR." Named for the 40th formulation of a water "displacement" compound, it was created in 1953 at the Rocket Chemical Company, in San Diego. Now it can be applied to fused-and-otherwise-stuck kazoos, to rocket them off into stratospheres of blazing success.

Care and Maintenance of the Kazooist

Lip Fatigue

Lip fatigue may be prevented by pacing yourself. Practice for short periods, gradually lengthening the sessions as you strengthen your embouchure muscles (see page 37) and build your endurance threshold.

Labial irritation (numbness from excessive vibration), a common malady of comb-and-tissue-paper artists, is virtually nonexistent among kazooists due to the superior ergonomic design of the instrument.

Chapping, Chafing, and Blistering

Lip balm is commonly used to relieve blistered, chapped, or cracked lips. For soft and supple hands, skin cream may be used, although only in moderation. Otherwise, an oil slick may form on the instrument, resulting in tongue slippage. A favorite remedy for hand chafing and chapping is a medicated ointment originally intended for cows with chapped udders.

Kazooists use it for protection against sunburn, windburn, and chafing.

Diet

Directly before an important performance, it is strongly recommended that abstinence from certain items be observed. Beer, chili, garlic, or other dyspeptic foods should be avoided, unless hiccoughing is a desired effect in the music.

Canadian and North Country Considerations

According to Canadian columnist Liz Braun-DeMarco (*Toronto Sun*), "It is illegal in all eight provinces to make any Canadian laugh out loud in winter. It is simply too frigid to waste the natural resources required to breathe in and out in this @#*& weather." This clearly rules out winter kazooing in the North Country.

CHAPTER THREE

RUDIMENTS

First Rule of Kazooing

The first rule of kazooing is knowing when *not* to kazoo. When *not* to kazoo is when it is someone else's turn or when someone else (such as your boss, teacher, leader, or co-kazooist) is talking.

The technical term for this is "tacit" (tă'sit) kazooing—which means you remain silent. It is also known as common sense, if bodily harm or threats are involved in requests to abstain from kazooing. "Tutti" (tōōt'ie), on the other hand, means everyone can jump right in.

Operating Instructions

1. Place larger end in mouth.

2. Keep fingers and thumbs out of mouth and clear of turret or other aperture areas.

3. Hum (DO NOT blow).

Note: If instrument fails to activate, loudly say the word "doo" into the larger end. Dooing into the turret may activate a particularly stubborn membrane. (If the instrument still does not respond properly, you're in trouble. You may have a broken hummer.)

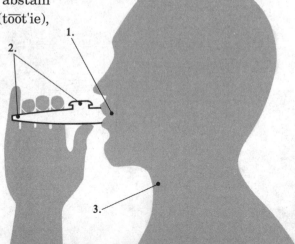

Starting Young: Home Schooling or Professional Instruction?

If the kazooist does not have access to high quality professional instruction or Kazoo University (Kazoo U.) online training, it is preferable to have home schooling with *The Complete How to Kazoo* as text.

Embouchure

The embouchure, or accurate positioning of the lips, is important to correct

kazooing. Assume a natural expression without smile, keeping the lips soft and flexible. Maintain that relaxed position, and open the center of the lips slightly, just enough to accommodate the kazoo.

Never exaggerate the position, as in the "Extreme Pucker," or stretch the mouth rigidly, as in the "Smile or Smirk Position."

The Smile or Smirk (incorrect)

Extreme Pucker (incorrect)

Ready Position (correct)

Jerry Darvin

Correct Hand Positions

#1—Basic

If right-handed, place the tips of the fingers of your right hand on top of the instrument, with your thumb grasping the barrel comfortably underneath. If left-handed, use the fingers of your left hand as indicated at right. If ambidextrous, toss a coin.

#2—Concert Style

Place the fingers of both hands on top of the barrel, placing thumbs underneath to balance, as in Position #1.

The fingering, of course, is purely decorative, since kazoo finger holes are either nonexistent or nonfunctional.

#3—"Wah-Wah" Position

This position is often used for jazz, since it graduates the sound and varies the shading. It is more traditionally used for harmonica.

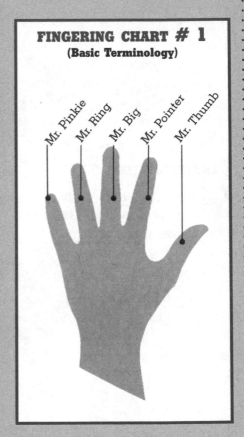

FINGERING CHART # 1
(Basic Terminology)

Mr. Pinkie — Mr. Ring — Mr. Big — Mr. Pointer — Mr. Thumb

#4—"No Hands" or "Expert"
The expert kazooist may choose this position particularly during passages requiring page turning or hand choreography.

Note: Fingers are not to be placed in facial apertures adjacent to your instrument, particularly during a concert performance.

FINGERING CHART # 2
(Especially useful
for country-western music)

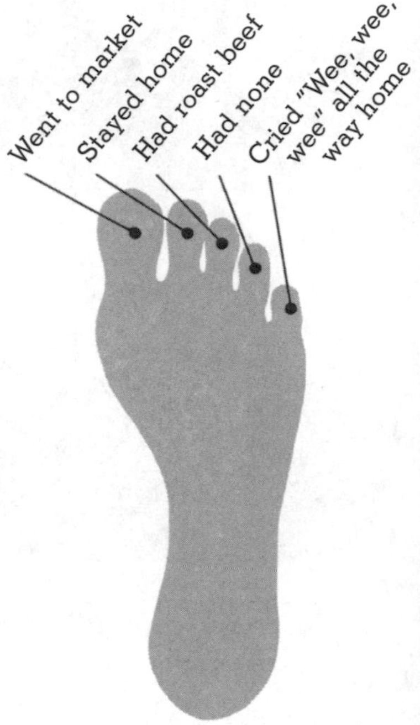

Went to market

Stayed home

Had roast beef

Had none

Cried "Wee, wee, wee" all the way home

Faux fingering and other imperspicuous esoterica

There are innumerable studies on achieving proper pinky placement for stringed-instrument bowing (although there are few for foot fingerings), which can be applied with the same amount of relevance to right or left pinky placement for kazooing.

The controversy in pianodom is over pinkie position in "straight" vs. "bent" pinkies for accelerated finger action. Kazooists may likewise advocate either or neither, since fingering is only decorative (faux) rather than functional.

Kazooing for the Musically Marginal

To begin your mastery of kazooing, first activate your kazoo (see page 36), select a comfortable pitch, follow directions for each exercise in this section, and practice where no one else is. The directions for refining your technique include suggested practice tunes. These songs, primarily simple tunes,

are well known and part of anyone's repertoire for singing and whistling in the shower. Until you become proficient in kazoo sounds, hum tunes into your instrument using the beginner syllables on page 50. For those without perceptible musical ability, take heart from the words of Ulysses S. Grant, who is reported to have said, "I only know two tunes. One of them is 'Yankee Doodle' and the other isn't." Both can be played on the kazoo.

Deactivating the Instrument

Parents, teachers, school bus drivers, co-workers, military officers, and other officials, be advised that kazoos can be instantly deactivated (disarmed and rendered harmless) by removing the resonating membrane from the turret.

Advanced Kazoo Techniques

Kazooists are occasionally met with mockery from the untutored, so it is important to remember that the kazoo is every bit as dignified as the person playing it. The kazoo band is also greater than the hole, which constitutes most of its parts. In general, if the kazooist chooses to do silly things, certainly it is a recognized and acceptable choice with this fun-time instrument. Remember that every day, most people do remarkably silly things without realizing it. A savvy kazooist recognizes silly when he/she sees it and is able to alter his/her behavior at will.

Therefore, kazoo without trepidation (fearlessly). Throw criticism (self- and otherwise) to the winds, and do not forget the public's insatiable appetite for mediocrity. After all, only the talentless are always at their best.

Spell it out for yourself. There is no stupid in kazoo. Above all, the kazoo is an auxiliary instrument, the perfect do-it-yourself instrument, amplifying whatever unique and personal ability you bring to it.

Arranging Music for Kazoo

I f the music has no spaces (rests) between the notes, this leaves no place to breathe. If the notes extend too high or too low for your singing range, you are also in trouble. Certain adjustments must be made to accommodate these problems, such as adding rests, bending the rhythm, or transposing notes into more convenient octaves. Kazooists call this "arranging." Musical purists call this atrocious.

Melody and Harmony

I n the study of music, great amounts of space are allotted to dissertation on musical form. For the purpose of kazooing, it would probably suffice to describe melody as notes laid

out horizontally. When notes are piled up vertically, they make a chord. In kazoo music, a chord presumes there is more than one kazooist. Otherwise, it is not a possibility, unless the kazoo is broken. If the chord is pleasing, it is harmony; if it is not pleasing, it is discord. Anyone wishing to dispute the technical accuracy of this should feel free to do so, keeping in mind, however, that there is only so much technical jargon the ordinary kazooist can tolerate and still be able to function. Oversimplification is always dangerous but, in this case, absolutely essential.

Written Kazoo Music

If you can't read regular music, you can't read kazoo music either. The classic diatonic scale is based on the "do-re-me-fa-sol-la-ti-do" tones, as most folks learned from *The Sound of Music.* If there is more than one kazooist, some semblance of this tonal system will be required. For this reason, you will need to hum by yourself or else learn to follow conventional organized musical patterns. If you are musically untutored, hum something you know or stay with unitone kazooing.

Most kazoo music has three parts: a beginning, a middle, and an end. The exceptions are Kazoobert's *Unfinished Symphony,* which has a beginning, and John Cage's *4'33"* (four and a half minutes of silence), which has nothing.

SECONDARY USES FOR A KAZOO

- As splints for small animals with injured legs
- As alarms for inexpensive smoke detectors

- As xylophones (lash kazoos together and hit them with Tootsie Pops)
- As miniature napkin rings

ESSENTIAL MUSIC NOTATION

space does not allow for an entire course in music theory, but there are a few basics that kazooists should know:

This is the **treble, or G, clef sign**. If you are humming music written in this clef, you should be female, a male doing falsetto, or a 17th-century castrato.

This is the **bass, or F, clef,** which is the range where the fellows should sing (or an occasional female, such as Carol Channing and the like).

This is a symbol of extreme importance to kazooists, since it means "STOP," "THE END," "IT'S OVER!"

Marking Time

Kazooists often don't count, so here is an easy method:

> Peach (whole note)
> Pie, pie (half note)
> Ap-ple, ap-ple (quarter notes)
> Huck-le-ber-ry, huck-le-ber-ry (eighth notes)
> Blue-ber-ry (triplets)

REASONS FOR KAZOOING

Kazooists are often asked the question "Why do you kazoo?" There is no need to dignify such a question with a lengthy reply. Instead, a well-chosen short retort will rid you of the questioner and allow you to get back to serious practicing.

I kazoo because:

1. It's there.
2. It requires no prior experience.
3. It's a wonderful leveler, making the finest singers sound no better or worse than I do.
4. The harmonica class was full.
5. Everyone should be an expert at something and this field is wide open.
6. I bought one by mistake and the store wouldn't take it back.

Safety Rules for Kazooing

- Place tape around mouthpiece to prevent chipping of teeth when using No-Hands technique.

- Do not persistently play the kazoo within earshot of those who are not true appreciators. It may lead to personal assault and bodily harm.

- Do not inhale through kazoo unless passage is clear of dust, lint, or other debris.

- Never stick the kazoo up your nose. Production of the nasal tone quality is sufficient using normal methods.

- Do not walk or run while playing unless supervised and under appropriate circumstances, such as playing in a marching band.

- In areas of subfreezing temperatures, use plastic kazoos, since a metal kazoo could become permanently affixed to your lips and/or tongue.

- Avoid sticking your fingers in the smaller end of the kazoo unless you have very tiny fingers or you wish to leave the kazoo indefinitely on your tip. If stuck, you may use soap to remove the instrument,

but this can cause soggy membrane and can also leave an unpleasant aftertaste.

- Do not use a metal kazoo outdoors during a thunderstorm or other natural phenomena accompanied by lightning.

Kazoo as I say, not as I doo!

Conducting Methodology (Pointers)

The conductor's baton doesn't have to be the sorcerer's wand; a sensible stick will do, provided it is attached to a competent wizard. Time is of the essence in conducting, so here is a shortcut to knowledge:

- *4/4 Time* (Floor, wall, wall, ceiling) Point baton down toward the floor, then toward left wall, right wall, then ceiling. Got that? Then repeat until you're done.

- *2/4 Time* (Floor, ceiling) Point baton toward the floor, then up toward the ceiling.

- *Slow Triple Time* (Floor, wall, ceiling) Point baton to the floor, right wall, ceiling.

- *Fast Triple Time* (Floor, float). For waltzes and so on, point down to the floor, then float up. Up, down, like a bouncing ball (or maybe a yo-yo).

At Home on the Kazoo Range

Speaking range bears no relation to kazooing range. To determine your kazooing range, try singing. On the whole, most women are altos or mezzo-sopranos and most men are baritones.

Note: For ensemble kazooing, basses are the hardest to locate. Being the most sought-after tends to spoil them, making them difficult to deal with, but you'll have to put up with that if you want the full range of vocal sounds.

Pitch

The kazooist with good pitch should be forewarned that only diligent practice in listening will develop his or her ear for kazoo pitches. Expert kazooists use the "arbitrary or discretionary" pitch method. Whatever pitch you

choose will produce a bombardment of sound with such complex overtones that it will be hard to tell what the original tonal center might have been. For this reason, the experienced kazooist aims for the center of the tone, makes a good approach for a layup, and hopes for the best on the rebound. The result is sort of a "rim shot."

Articulation

Because of the delightfully murky quality of kazoo sonorities, articulation and clear diction are of the utmost importance to the kazooist. Special attention and much practice should be devoted to the art of overarticulation, in other words, exaggerating the syllables to be sung, spoken, or tongued. The following is a basic vocabulary of kazoo articulation syllables for the beginner:

doo, dee, dum, da, ta, tu, tum

Once you have mastered these, you should proceed to the more advanced list of authorized kazoo sounds on page 52.

Muting & Pianissimo

For romantic passages or performing in areas with noise-restrictive codes or other dangers, it is possible to mute the sound and make pitches very soft (pianissimo) by turning the instrument around and humming into the smaller end.

This is not practical in fast passages if soft pitches alternate rapidly with loud ones, since logistics would be awkward. In this case, it's best to work with a second kazooist. While you execute muted pitches into the smaller end of the kazoo, your partner plays the louder notes into the regular mouthpiece. This can be done on two kazoos or one, depending on familiarity with your accompanist.

UNITONE PRACTICE TUNES FOR ARTICULATION

Practice examples 1 through 3. Then practice them using the sounds and articulations in the box on page 52. Any or all of the sounds may be used separately or in combination.

Example 1

Sing: Doo   Doo   Doo   Doo   Doo   Doo

Example 2

Count: 1, 2, 3, 4   1, 2, 3, 4   Doo Doo Doo Doo   Doo

Example 3

Sing: Doo Doo   Doo   Dum Dum   Dum

AUTHORIZED LIST OF ACCEPTABLE SOUNDS AND ARTICULATIONS TO PRACTICE ON THE KAZOO

a	glortch	lurp	op	snam	wah
ach	glurp	mmm-	org	snap	wah
ah	ha	mmm	pip	snart	wirp
am	hee	moff	pitoot	snat	woo
ap	heep	mom	poo	snit	woom
arg	herp	mop	poop	snort	wrrp
ark	hmmm-	morf	pop	snorg	wub
arp	mmm	morn	porp	sorg	wum
atch	hmmm-	morp	prrup	sploing	wuz
blaft	mmm	mos	ptui	sss	ya
blah	mm	mrp	quarg	ssst	yoo
blanft	ho	muff	quash	ta	yub
blant	hum	mugort	que	ta-ka	yum
blap	ich	mum	rep	tcht	yup
blat	icht	mump	retch	ti	zah
dah	ka	mus	rivet	tra	zeb
dee	karp	nah	romp	tra-la	zedah
doo	kritch	nich	rop	tretch	zen
doom	krrp	nit	rot	trrt	zib
doomp	la	nnn	rrrp	tst	zit
doop	lee	nom	rrrr	tu-ka	zoo
dum	li	norp	rrt	tum	zoom
ecch	lo	nortch	sam	tum-	
echk	lol	num	scam	tum	
erg	lop	og	slop	ugh	
erp	lul	oh	slorp	urg	
glitch	lum	ooo	slump	utch	
glort	lun	oop	snag	wah	

Advanced Sounds

blang	gurnp
bzownt	krunchle
bzznt	krukle
chank	noit
chunka	oomph
dang	ploin
dink	poif
dit	poit
doik	pwang
doing	shkling
fak	skitch
fap	skrotch
finitich	slmet
foidoip	sluk
foing	snark
fong	snorkel
foompt	spap
foong	splang
fot	splork
furd	spritz
fwat	sprong
fween	swart
fweep	thaff
glit	turg
gloig	twing
glorg	zickik
gluk	zooka
gort	

Another method is to kazoo with the turret upside down, which creates a muting effect (except for any pets underfoot) by projecting sound waves toward your feet.

Dynamics

"Dynamics" is the technical term for how loud or soft the sound is (musical volume). If you play the kazoo too loudly (fortissimo), the membrane might break. If you play too softly (pianissimo), the membrane does not vibrate properly. So the kazooist aims for consistency in the middle dynamic range, striving always for mediocrity.

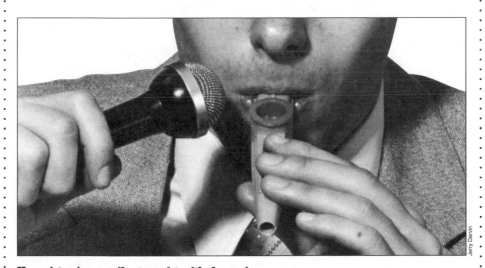

Jerry Darvin

Kazooist using a mike to assist with dynamics.

An excellent practice tune for dynamics is "John Jacob Jingleheimer Schmidt."

Vocalization

The dedicated kazooist may extend his or her range through the diligent practice of vocalization exercises. Pronounce the following syllables, first without the kazoo and then a second time pronouncing them into the instrument.

Level 1. eh ēe ah ōh ooo
Level 2. ah eh ēe ōh ooo
Level 3. ēe ī ēe ī ō

Once you have reached level 3, you are prepared for folk and farm kazooing.

Voice Projection

Effective voice projection will enable you to reach the greatest number of listeners in the shortest period of time. When projecting their voices, opera and classical singers use head tones. Jazz and pop singers use throat and chest tones. Kazooists use anything they can.

Perform frequent repetitions of the musical scales (do, re, mi, fa, sol, la, ti, do) with the assistance of a friend or loved one. Ask your helper to keep backing away as you repeat the scales, requiring you to increase your projection so that he or she can always hear you. Helpers should not be permitted to back off into a car and drive away.

Electric Kazooing

Kazooists experiment with electronic kazoos of various descriptions, but it is yet to be proven that electrified ones are superior to regular ones properly aimed at microphones or other amplifying devices.

Kazoo sounds are produced by voice activation of the resonating membrane and resulting dispersion of antagonistic vibration mostly within the turret

(trumpet collection device). Thus, it makes little sense to place an electronic pickup device attached directly to the turret. It may fail to collect extraneous vibrations that spritz backwards from the resonator into the barrel, thus missing this delicious afterburn of peripheral buzzing. For pure and economical results, aim an unadulterated (plain) turret at a microphone, and let 'er rip.

If true kazooing is irrelevant and you need to affect a hi-tech appearance to impress others, you can plug yourself (with basic safety precautions) into almost any audio device with a connector attached to a safety cap on the kazoo turret.

Breathing

And why not! Some variation of the "inhale/exhale" (in/out) breathing technique is a primary requisite for kazooing. Respiration experts estimate that the average kazooist takes 20,000 to 25,000 breaths a day. The volume and number of breaths per minute (and exhaled carbon dioxide that benefits plant life) will vary with the size of the kazooist and the level of activity.

The average concert kazooist breathes approximately 15 times per minute.[3] The approximate total volume of recycled breaths can be calculated by multiplying the exhale formulation by 2 to incorporate the function of intake.

While it is well known to musicologists that, among aerophone

[3]www.cchem.berkeley.edu/~chem1a/ fall95/ discussion/week1/takeabreathsoln.htm

$$\frac{0.5\, L\, of\, air}{breath} \times \frac{15\, breaths}{min.} \times \frac{60\, min}{hr.} \times \frac{24\, hr.}{day} = \frac{1.08 \times 10^{4}\, L\, of\, air}{day}$$

> **Two kazoos are not necessarily better than one
> if one kazooist is musically marginal.**

instrumentalists (wind players), maximum air pressure is required for the bombardon (German tuba) or American sousaphone, the kazoo has not been as well studied.

Whereas the sound-generating medium of the aerophone is an enclosed column of air set in vibration by the compressed lips of the brass player, the kazoo, as a membranophone, produces its sound through voice-activated bombardment of a stretched membrane. No one is sure how much air pressure is required to produce sound without jeopardizing the integrity of the membrane (breaking it), but usually the audience will register outer limits of tolerance (complaints) before this occurs.

Breath Control

The basic technique for breathing is, of course, *in* and *out*. However, notes should be produced only on the *out*-take, unless you are striving to produce a piggy snort (page 72).

*Practice exercise
for breath control:*

1. Place a "party blowout" (the paper party favor that unrolls when you blow into it) firmly into the smaller end of the kazoo.

2. Suck in a huge breath, inhaling through the mouth (not the nose) and expanding the abdominal area. Do not raise shoulders when inhaling.

3. Holding on to the party favor, blow out and sustain the breath, keeping the paper tail expanded for as long as possible.

4. If dizziness results, discontinue practice and take a vacation.

Extensive breath control practice is crucial to proper renditions of such classics as:
"I Know an Old Lady Who Swallowed a Fly"
"Twelve Days of Christmas"
"Green Grass Grew All Around"
"100 Bottles of Beer on the Wall"
"In Poland There's an Inn"

Fry Tones

The bottom tone of the bass can be lowered (although not necessarily improved) by using a singing technique referred to as "fry tones." Pick the lowest note possible and then use the throat to pronounce the syllables

"WRahahahah," imitating the sound of a creaking door. Fry tones are useful for producing a bottom note lower than your ordinary capacity or for occasions requiring sustained growling, such as pep rallies and football games.

Vibrato

Vibrato is the wavy variation of sound within the tone that gives it texture. It adds colorful over-tones by changing the sound waves and is a technique used by singers and many instrumental-ists to enhance their tone quality.

Vibrato may be achieved by varying the breath using muscu-lar control of the diaphragm (stomach) or by vibrating the lip or jaw.

An attempt should be made to keep the vibrato in even pulses, the most pleasant effect.

Practice exercise:
The kazooist should breathe from the diaphragm, choosing a single pitch and pronouncing the syllables "taah-ah" into the kazoo. This is known as the "Santa Claus laugh." It produces a wavy quality within the sound, enhancing the richness of the sonorousness. Snow White's diminutive friends sing a song that the kazooist can perform to practice vibrato—"Heigh Ho, Heigh Ho, It's Off to Work We Go." "Greensleeves," Brahms's "Lullaby," and "Up on the Rooftops" may be used to prac-tice more advanced stages.

> **Better to remain silent and be thought a fool than to kazoo badly and remove all doubt.**

Rhythm and Meter

Rhythm and meter are different things, but the distinction probably will not matter much to you as a solo kazooist.

Where there is more than one kazooist, however, it is desirable to know basic musical counting. Not knowing how long each note should last and how it fits can create hostility among the members of your musical group. For example, if you hold the note too long, you will overlap onto someone else's note and end after everybody else is finished. If you don't hold your note long enough, you will come in on the next one too soon and cause another collision situation, skipping past everybody else's part to get to the end before they do.

To avoid these potential musical embarrassments, find a patient kazoo partner and practice "Row, Row, Row Your Boat" as a round, with frequent repetitions, until you have mastered musical counting. Other practice rounds include "White Coral Bells," "Make New Friends," and "Why Doesn't My Goose Sing as Well as Thy Goose." Better yet, stick to solo kazooing, where you don't have to worry about stepping on anyone else's toes or notes.

Double and Triple Tonguing

Standard instrumental articulation for single tonguing (syllables you tongue into the kazoo) includes "ta," "du," or "tu," but hardly any musician does this for fast passages, because single tonguing cannot be reproduced quickly enough. Instead they use double or triple tonguing.

Standard instrumental articulation for double tonguing is "ta-ka," "du-ka," "du-ga," or "tu-ka." Triple tonguing is just like double tonguing, only faster. Triple tonguing requires the use of an additional syllable: "ta-ka-ta," "du-ka-ta," or "du-ga-da."

This technique is crucial for the proper execution of Chopin's "Minute Waltz," which takes an expert pianist at least 98 seconds to complete. "The Fifty-Nine

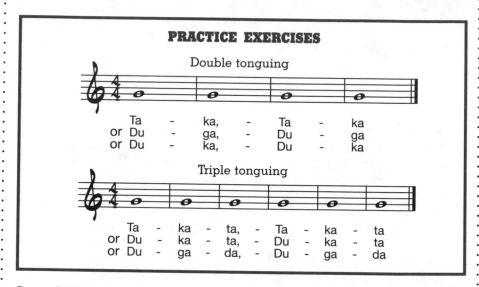

PRACTICE EXERCISES

Double tonguing

Ta	-	ka,	-	Ta	-	ka
or Du	-	ga,	-	Du	-	ga
or Du	-	ka,	-	Du	-	ka

Triple tonguing

Ta	-	ka	-	ta,	-	Ta	-	ka	-	ta
or Du	-	ka	-	ta,	-	Du	-	ka	-	ta
or Du	-	ga	-	da,	-	Du	-	ga	-	da

Second Waltz" for kazoos can be completed in as little as 55 seconds by using the double or triple tonguing technique.

Practice exercises:
Choose whichever of these syllables are easiest for you to repeat and practice the repetition, using "ta-ka," "du-ka," or "du-ga." Use any comfortable pitch.

Flutter and Slap Tonguing

Flutter tonguing is a rapid whirring of the tongue against the teeth with the sound of a rolled "thrrrrr," something like a Scotsman with his tongue stuck in a lisp. It is one of the techniques that great teachers claim either you can do or you can't, but whatever the case, it can't be taught. It doesn't seem to be related to the inherited genetic ability to curl your tongue in the center. Flutter tonguing between two pitches can create a trill-like effect. Trills are used in marching band music, specifically in standard flute and clarinet parts adapted for the kazoo. This technique is also particularly useful for bird and animal calls.

Slap tonguing, a sloppier version of flutter tonguing, involves greatly extending your tongue while producing a much coarser sound. The "Blue Danube Waltz" is greatly enhanced by slap tonguing—dum, dee, da, dum, THUCK-THUCK, THUCK-THUCK . . . and so forth.

Glissandos

Glissandos are transitions from one note to another through the use of a series of passing tones. The type of glissando you will use on the kazoo requires the player to gliss, smooth, or glide over all the notes between the two indicated. How you get between the two notes (whether you buzz, bend, gliss, rip, slide, or bump) is of little relevance, as long as you arrive at your destination. The easiest and most successful glissando technique for the kazooist is the "smear." Simply start on the beginning note and smear up or down to the indicated target note.

Jazz and blues kazooists make regular use of the bent tone glissando. Advanced kazooists can practice a glissando technique in Gershwin's "Rhapsody in Blue."

Balalaika Effect

The sound of the balalaika, a Russian lutelike instrument, can be simulated by tonguing on the kazoo, using rapid repetition of the articulation "lu-lu-lu," "addle-addle-addle," or "doodle-oodle-oodle," depending on your esthetic preference.

The balalaika effect can be used as a vocal accompaniment, without kazoo, propelling the tongue outside the mouth in a rapid side-to-side rotation while pronouncing the same syllables

RHAPSODY IN KAZOO

In 1924, George Gershwin performed the world premiere of his *Rhapsody in Blue* with the Paul Whiteman Orchestra in New York. The score for orchestra and piano was arranged by Ferdinand Grofé (composer of *Grand Canyon Suite*) for the basic Whiteman Orchestra (trumpets, trombones, saxophones, piano, violins, string bass, banjo, and percussion). In a later arrangement for a large orchestra, Grofé also added two French horns, B-flat clarinet, oboe, tuba, celesta, and "muted kazoo." History is somewhat fuzzy on who kazooed and how he/she muted it. Stuffed a sock in the turret? Parked gum on the resonator? Grocery bag over the kazooist's head? Played upside down to send vibrations into the floor? What?

or using the pronunciation "blhlhlhlhl." Shaking the head from side to side helps keep the motion perpetual. The visual image is greatly enhanced by strumming an imaginary instrument while producing the vocalized sounds.

"Those Were the Days" and "Song of the Volga Boatmen" are excellent practice songs for balalaika effect.

Overriding Principle of Serendipity

Serendipity is different from ordinary dippity, dippity-doo, or zippity doo-dah, which are something else altogether. Serendipity is the act of finding something fortunate or delightful while expecting something else. This happens to kazooists often so if it works, pretend it was on purpose.

Utilitarian Kazooing: Who Let the Kazoos Out?

Utilitarian kazooing has the dual purpose of delighting the kazooist with his or her own artistry while accomplishing a useful function such as calling birds or animals. In the mouth of an accomplished kazooist, this can be achieved with astonishing success.

Chickening Out

Chicken sounds can be made using the syllables "errach, bawlk, bawlk." It's best to perform the "bawlk" beginning on a low pitch with the "b" and rising to a higher pitch for the throat-catching "awlk." An "rrrr-rr-rr-rr-errr" repetition will give you the barnyard wakeup call, a rooster's cry.

Seagull Trailing

The kazooist can easily imitate the seagull by performing a screaming "eee" starting on the high pitch and trailing off in a downward bent pitch.

Turkey Calling

Here's a handy seasonal call, popular every Thanksgiving. A double- or single-reed (free mirliton) turkey caller is commercially available, but a skilled kazooist can produce a perfectly satisfactory call.

The turkey aficionado is able to produce the entire turkey repertoire on kazoo, including huffing, yelps, putts, purrs, clucks, whistles, keekee run, cackle, and the ever popular gobble.

The easiest call to master is the basic "bllullulp," pronouncing the sound rapidly on a high pitch. This call in itself is suffi-cient to call any domestic and most wild turkeys.

It is important to note that turkey calling should not be attempted in the rain. Turkeys are so stupid that when they look up to find the caller, they do so with open mouths and can drown as a result. Rain also

> **If it walks like a duck and quacks like a duck,
> it's a duck—or possibly a kazooist.**

results in soggy vibrators for the kazooist, or even rust, so on the whole, it is best to wait for more favorable weather conditions.

Duck Calls

Commercially made duck calls force air past the reed, causing it to vibrate and produce a buzzing sound. The kazooist can produce the same effect by enunciating through the nose on the syllables "quack," "rrack," or "qvack." Many modern duck callers imitate the Aflac Insurance Company duck call, honking the nasal exhaled syllables "aaaf-lak."

Edgar Allan Crow Talk

The crow's close cousin, the raven, is most noted for outbursts of

"Nevermore!" in Edgar Allan Poe's poetry. Nonfictional crows do not say this (nor do real ravens), staying with annoying hoarse repetitions of "caw, caw."

If you call crows, be forewarned that you may find yourself set upon by a whole passle of excessively unattractive Corvid family relatives, including grackles, starlings, blackbirds, jays, magpies, nutcrackers, or even overseas choughs. Actually, a clump of crows is referred to as a "murder" of crows, a reference to a habit of killing their own for reasons best known to other crows. On the whole, I recommend calling some other, more attractive species.

Loon Laughing and Lamenting

This is most effective in desolate northern areas frequented by nearly no one except wildlife. There are four basic calls: the hoot; the tremolo (resembling insane laughter); the eerie wail; and the yodel (males only). The tremolo is the most intriguing ("oo-ahhh-hoo"). It indicates agitation or fear and starts with a low-pitched "oo" and rises on ascending pitches to open up on the syllable "ah," with a slight warble. This is buttoned at the end with a rapidly placed, lower-pitched "hoo."

Wild, Domestic, and Pirate Parrots

Parrots come in a remarkable array of species, all of which seem to talk, although only a few of them speak English. Most make extremely unpleasant squawks, shrieks, and screams, well suited to kazooing.

Like their owners, pirate parrots of the talking type often have an assortment of vocabulary words, some of which are clearly socially unacceptable. Polite domesticated parrots are more likely to say such things as "What?" or whistle tunes, although some ask independent questions, which is unnerving if you are expecting only imitation. Parrot sounds can be as simple as the traditional squawk beginning with a high-pitched throat propelled "AWK! Polly wants a cracker" or an ascending screech of "Rrr-akkk!"

Who Gives a Hoot?

Owls are nocturnal and few venture out during daylight hours (owl and professional

musician naptime), so there is little practical purpose to hooting any time except at night. The easiest call is the barn owl, two "oo"s followed by a short burst "uh" and elongated "oo" to finish ("oo-oo-uh-oooo").

For variation, the great horned owl has several calls, including "hoo-hoo-hooooo," which can be greatly enhanced by adding glottal vibrato. The shrieking call is a high-pitched screaming "eeee," uttered on the breath intake rather than by exhaling.

Swan Songs

The "swan song" is described in mythology as a thrilling and heart-wrenching melody, sung just as life departs the swan deathbed. In real life, swans are apt to snort, grunt, rattle, cackle, bugle, hiss, and utter high-pitched cries that sound like something between baying hounds and Canada geese, but there seems to be no singing. On the chance that the mortality legend is true, do not put yourself or any impressionable swans in jeopardy of premature expiration by testing the death cry.

Woolgathering
(Sheep Calls)

Repelling sheep is infinitely easier than attracting them. Their instinct is to avoid kazooists, unless there is a sheep dog, louder kazooist, or other feared force behind them.

The recommended technique is to position a team of dog-barking kazooists behind the flock to get them going in the direction of the single sheep-calling kazooist. That kazooist attracts them by using sheep language while holding food (sheep bait). A throat-uttered "baa-aa" or "maa-anhh" on a single broken pitch is about as complicated as sheep language gets. The exceptions are the "Unemployed Counting Sheep" of the Serta Mattress Company, all of whom speak English and are numbered so you can tell to whom you are speaking.

Getting Someone's Goat

To the untrained ear, goats sound much like sheep. However, while the sheep noise "maanhh" comes from the top of the mouth with lips together, goats stick out their tongue, producing more of a nasal "aaan-anhhh"[4] (Nigerian dwarf goats have been observed to follow this technique for countless hours. We are not sure about other species.)

[4]Primary observations by Whitney Stewart in Africa, 2004.

- As a lightning rod, when placed (without kazooist) on the roof of a barn
- To lead cavalry charges in military units that lack bugles
- As taxi horns in underdeveloped countries
- As peanut butter or other sandwich spreaders
- As replacement fasteners for elongated keg-type buttons on duffel coats

- As nose makeup for Cyrano de Bergerac role

Going to the Dogs

Dog calling can be accomplished by whistling or name-calling in a limited pitch range, since the kazooist cannot reach the higher ranges perceived by the canine ear. If the dog is conditioned to Skinner stimulus/response behavior, the animal will understand your call as meaning food and/or attention and will automatically respond positively.

Yipping and yapping in dog language means "Give me attention!"—the equivalent of "Hey! Hey! Hey!" repeated to the point of exasperation. Barking and howling are more complex and scientists are not yet entirely sure what this means to the dog, so be cautious vocalizing, unless the nearby dog is known to be friendly or confined in some manner (leash or cage). "Ruff," "rrrrr," "woof," and "ah-ooou" (howling) are standard communication; low-pitched growling and direct eye contact are not advised.

Pig Calling

Hollering "sue-eeee," beginning on a low-pitched "sue" and rising to the hair-raising "eee" strung out in plaintive legato or with staccato cutoff, can be heard at great distances. This is particularly interesting to pigs, although not well understood by others.

Piggy Snort

The piggy snort is produced by rapid and simultaneous air intake through the nose and mouth in a staccato snort. This not only intrigues pigs, but produces a splendid drum roll-off effect, when employed rhythmically to begin marches or other military events. Pig squeals can be made by inhaling while articulating "eeee," but this method has few known musical applications.

FROGGY PRACTICE TUNE

Sing the lyrics the first time through. Kazoo the second time. This may be used as a solo or a three-part round.

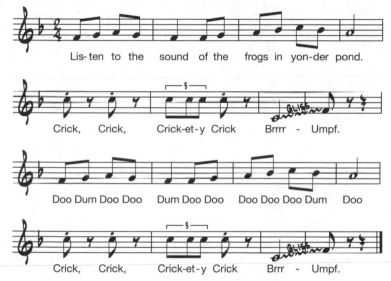

Lis-ten to the sound of the frogs in yon-der pond.

Crick, Crick, Crick-et-y Crick Brrrr - Umpf.

Doo Dum Doo Doo Dum Doo Doo Doo Doo Doo Dum Doo

Crick, Crick, Crick-et-y Crick Brrrr - Umpf.

Frog Noises

You don't need to have green flippers to sound as if you've been around a swamp. A truly fine tree-frog sound requires a soprano kazooist, although lower voices can approximate the effect in falsetto. The sound is made by the articulation "breep," rolled on a flutter tongue from a lower pitch up to top pitch and repeated two or three times. Other frog sounds such as "brrap," "rrack," and "churragarrroom," are better suited to the bass kazooist.

One note of caution: Overusing these sounds should be avoided, since it may cause warts on the vocal cords.

Donkey Call

You will probably never have use for a donkey call—that is, unless prospecting for gold. Inhale on the syllable "hee" and exhale on "haw" for an effective donkey call. The *Grand Canyon Suite* by Grofé uses this effect nicely, as do several folk songs, of which "Old MacDonald Had a Farm" is the best known. Use the inhale/exhale technique for the "heehaw" syllables. Once you remember "Here a hee" (inhale on hee), "Here a haw" (exhale on haw), the rest is easy.

Moose Call

If you ever need to find a moose, your kazoo can come in handy. Commercially made moose callers may be purchased, but a perfectly acceptable sound can be achieved with a kazoo.

Before commencing, it is important to check your immediate area of the woods for moose in close proximity, and take care not to stand in the center of a path when calling.

The call itself is an extended "Ououhooohh." The initial bellow begins on a low pitch, rising slightly and then dropping in descending scale on the final "ooohh." The ending sometimes drops slowly, sometimes more sharply, and closely resembles the cry of a large wolf with a bass voice and severe intestinal difficulty.

An easier, alternative method is a simple "mmooo" like a cow, since moose seem to lack discrimination and farmers often complain moose are irrefutably attracted (and annoying) to cows.

Wolf Whistles and Moon Howling

Wolves in the animal kingdom both howl and yip, pointing their noses toward the moon. (We're not sure why all 32 subspecies of wolves participate in attempted communication with an uninhabited lunar body 238,000 miles away, but perhaps they know something we don't.) The traditional wolf howl is "ow-ooo-ooo," beginning low and rising to the spine-tingling "oo" sound that drops off into a final mournful "ew" ("oo"), sometimes in staggered steps that resemble a ragged arpeggio. When there is more than one howler, wolves do not choose to resonate on the same pitch as anyone else, so for authenticity in group vocalizing, pick different tones for howling.

The Bzst and the Zzt

Some experts claim that bees and kazooists both hum because they don't know the words. Whatever the reason, bee sounds are a natural on the kazoo. The

the rise of the "t" part of the sound on a pitch a half step higher.

Catch-all Caterwauls

"Meow" and "mew" and wailing "mrrr-owww"s are standard cat calling repertoire, along with the old favorite "Here Kitty, Kitty!" You may call felines by their given names, but they rarely come unless hungry and there is food involved. The most effective call is the sound of a can opener.

Human catcalling to indicate derision or disapproval is mostly employed at sporting events. The most socially acceptable version is "boo." However, unruly crowds sometimes impolitely deteriorate into more specific and inappropriate disdain concerning family heritage and mothers or sisters. The effectiveness of this hooligan behavior

"bzst" sound is begun with the "b" and quickly moves on to the "zst" syllable while the tongue vibrates in the central mouth cavity behind closed teeth. You must be careful not to cut off the air stream with the vibrating tongue.

For the "zzt" the experienced buzzer can begin a "zz" on a selected pitch and sharply accent

evolves with cultural changes and so is hard to follow. For example, in another generation, the catcall "Your mother wears army boots!" was construed as insulting, but it is now a source of pride and honor.

The most popular catcall to indicate disapproval is the Bronx cheer (see page 78).

Dating Calls

Attempts to categorize date types is similar to making up names to classify rock groups—ubersexual, metrosexual, heterosexual, homosexual, bisexual; sensitive, insensitive, or neutrosensitive (I see your pain, I just don't feel it); feminist, macho; Mr. or Ms. Right; Mr. or Ms. That's Close Enough. Regardless, there are still only the same three basic varieties (male, female, and undecided).

To appeal to the primitive instincts of any date, try a Tarzan call. Starting on a low-pitched "ah" in your ugliest chest tone, raise an interval of a 5th and yodel on "eeee-ah" (alternating broken pitches between chest and head tones) and drop back to a final deep throat "ah."

Novelty Kazooing

This category is largely experimental in nature and is useful mostly for free-form party kazooing or novelty effects. Some may be appended to musical compositions for emphasis, but generally these noises are used as sound effects rather than being melodically employed.

The Bronx Cheer

The Bronx cheer is a sound usually used in crowds to indicate disapproval (it is also known as the raspberry). It is particularly useful in the stands at baseball or football games. On kazoo, the technique requires an overbite in the embouchure, with the upper lip on top of the uptilted kazoo, the lower lip tucked under, and the tongue in the barrel of the kazoo. The kazooist buzzes the lips and tongue, pronouncing a motorized "th" sound and propelling it forward with the vibrating lips and tongue.

Hand choreography for the Bronx cheer is simple. Place

The double-handed Bronx cheer.

Jerry Darvin

your thumbs at the sides of your head and wiggle your fingers. An alternate thumb position is careful placement of the right or left thumb on the top of your nose and vigorously waving the fingers of that hand in a rippling effect.

The Doppler Effect

The Doppler effect is an apparent change in the frequency of the sound waves that occurs when the source of the sound and the receiver of the sound are in motion relative to each other. The kazooist can achieve this effect in one of two ways:

1. The listener and kazooist remain stationary while the kazooist recreates the illusion of approaching and receding sound by starting off softly, raising the pitch and intensity, finally fading off as if into the distance.

2. The listener remains stationary. The kazooist starts off a distance away and runs past the listener, keeping the sound at the same level throughout.

Note: The second approach is not recommended for kazooists, since it requires more physical conditioning than the first and involves some risk to the kazooist's well-being if he or she should stumble.

Antiphonal Kazooing
(Ensemble Echo Effect)

To enhance the monophonic sound of a single kazooist, add antiphonal effects with kazooists placed in different areas to kazoo in response to each other to create an echo effect.

If you have only one kazooist, you can achieve the same effect if you are in excellent physical condition.

1. Kazoo the opening phrase at one location.
2. Run to a second location and kazoo the same thing.
3. Run back to the original location and kazoo the next phrase from there.
4. Repeat as necessary.

Prime practice tunes are songs with parroted lyrics that can be repeated endlessly and may or may not bear repeating, such as "Oh, You Can't Get to Heaven," "Sippin' Cider through a Straw," "Oh, My Aunt Came Back from Timbuktu," "Little Sir Echo," and the like. Partner songs, including "Skip to My Lou," "Bow Belinda," and "Sandy Land," can also be sung separately or together.

Singing Bridges, Seat Belt Warning Signals, Watch Alarms, and Electronic Greeting Card Pitches

All of the above provide splendid opportunities for kazoo accompaniment, especially for kazooists on the road. Using the humming sound of car wheels on the bridge, the seat belt warning device, or watch alarm pitch, the kazooist selects the pitch an interval of a 3rd, a 5th, or an octave above to complete the chord. If you don't know music theory, pick a pitch and throw it in. If there is only a single kazooist, the most pleasing pitch is the interval of a 3rd over the starting pitch (root), since an open 5th gives a peculiar sound not well suited to much except medieval music. Electronic greeting cards that play tunes offer opportunities to either sing along or harmonize.

If you have no pitch whatsoever, stick with solo kazooing.

Sirens

American siren noises require a low-pitched whine ("oww") for the beginning, scooping up to a higher pitch and dropping back to fade out.

The European siren is a different sound entirely, encompassing

two pitches rotated back and forth. Using the basic articulation "ee-ah, ee-ah," the European version begins on a middle pitch with the "ee" sound, then drops down in pitch on the syllable "ah," and continues rotating monotonously between the two pitches "ee-ah, ee-ah," and so on.

To accompany the siren with the Doppler effect, begin either siren series softly (pianissimo),

gradually increasing the volume until you fade off into the distance. This is a lot of fun at parties but should not be used outdoors where it could create a traffic hazard. The new electronic sirens pose a challenge to all but the most expert kazooists.

Motor Noises

"Brroom," "brrum," and so on, with rolled articulation, can be used in endlessly varied motor imitations. Also useful is the throat squeal, the unrolled "rrrrr" sound familiar to any motorist who has ever slammed on the brakes for an abrupt stop in traffic. Explosion or smashing notes may also be added to this sequence of special effects. All of these are aided by the artful use of the microphone, especially for the explosion sound, usually produced by the rolling and blowing out of the syllable "prrwhwhwh," exploding the "prrr" and continuing to taper off with the softer "whwhwh" blowing sound.

Water Noises

By placing the smaller end of the kazoo barrel into water and playing into the wide end, a pleasing array of unusual effects can be achieved. Burbling, bubbling, and excellent "grracks"; "bllups" (with rolled *l*s) in addition to throat-produced gargling noises, such as "guh," "gah," and vibrated *g*s, are some useful water noises.

Do not inhale when your kazoo is submerged, since it ruins the resonator. A soggy vibrator will preclude any repetition of effective kazoo sounds after the intake.

Foghorn Alert

The foghorn is most effective for the bass kazooist. The "bah-ahhahh" articulation begins on a low pitch with the "bah," extending above to "ahh" and returning to the tonic (the same note you started on) with the second "ahh." This is repeated over and over again at five-second intervals.

Kazooists in coastal areas may want to check with local authorities to be sure that simulating fog horns will not be confusing to ships or violate maritime ordinances.

If a thing is worth kazooing, it's worth kazooing twice.

Backup Alarm Alert

The backing-up truck alarm sound may be used to warn your audience when you plan to play a tune backward. Before playing retrograde compositions, first turn your back to the audience, then emit a high-pitched "eep, eep, eep," repeated at regular intervals, to sound the alert.

Couch Potato Weather Watching

Rather than passively observing or listening to the weather on TV or radio, supply your own sound effects and music. Just as movies require mood music, add appropriate background sound to accompany the reporting weather person: "You Are My Sunshine," "Raindrops Are Falling on My Head," "Winter Wonderland," and so on can be used to accompany appropriate

forecasts. If the broadcaster already supplies music, hum along.

If you can't think of a tune, use a "sound comment" such as "sss-sss" for hot weather, "brr-rr" for blizzard, etc. If you are unable to come up with a creative sound, try talking into your instrument to add opinions such as "That's right" or "Oh, no," or some such helpful commentary.

The exception for all of this, of course, is during power outage events such as ice storms, hurricanes, and so on, when appliances are knocked out and you will have to supply your own information in addition to sound effects, unless you have a battery- or crank-operated radio. In this case, make up your own reports and accompany yourself.

Tandem Kazooing

For additional amplification, two or three kazoos may be taped together, end on end, to form one long tube with multiple turrets. The addition of a funnel at the escape-hole end of the tube will further enhance the sound projection, acting acoustically as

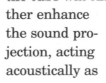

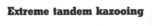

Extreme tandem kazooing

the bell of a brass or wind instrument does to disseminate sound
emitting from the end of the tube.

Double-Barreled Approach (Multiple Instruments)

Because of the kazoo's size,
more than one kazoo can
be played at a time, pro-
vided the player's lips can
wrap tightly enough around
the instruments to sufficiently
seal the air leakage. The use
of more than one instrument
looks impressive but adds little
to the musicality of the moment,
since the single kazooist can
produce a maximum of one set
of sounds at a time, no matter
how many instruments he or
she can accommodate in his or
her mouth.

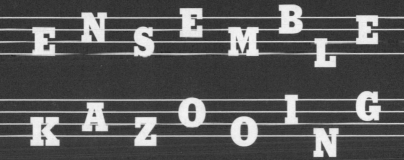

CHAPTER FOUR

ENSEMBLE KAZOOING

(Banding Together for More Perfect Harmony)

Kazoo Banding Is Natural Instinct

The final step for kazooists is deciding in what direction to kazoo. Kazooing cuts across all cultural barriers and is appropriate for all ages. The range and possibility for kazoo groups is virtually limitless. It seems to vary only according to the imagination and inclination of the kazooists.

Although kazooists may choose to join a group to form a more perfect union, freedom of choice in kazooing is held to be self-evident. The rights of the individual kazooist, including the rights to free speech, to following Kazoodaism as a way of life, the right to assemble, and to the assurance of a speedy and fair trial for any violation of local ordinances are guaranteed by law, at least for American kazooists. The independent kazooist who chooses individual expression rather than kazooing in a group is to be taken just as seriously as the group kazooist. The domestic kazooist who chooses to remain at home, in the kitchen, or with the children is to be no less respected than the ensemble or professional (working) kazooist. Freedom of kazooing is the rule rather than the exception.

KEEP AMERICA HUMMING

KEEP AMERICA humming

Jerry Darvin

Unibanding (groups of one)

The uniband is a group of one. An example is a one-person band with multiple instruments (often referred to as one-man-bands, popular among street musicians and mimes). The uniband genre is also well suited to the musically marginal, single-minded kazooist who prefers to remain an individual unit, apart from others because of personal safety concerns.

At the center of mediocrity in any field is the problem of dense population and overcrowding. A kazooist may choose unibanding to avoid jealousy and artistic conflict, assuring that his or her position will prevail, regardless of ability.

Ensemble Leadership (Kazookeeping)

It is the kazookeeper's duty to enthusiastically lead, follow, or get out of the way. If properly inspired, the group will use its collective creativity to go further than expectations could possibly envision.

Thus one of the duties of kazookeeping is to explain instances of excess enthusiasm to authorities or offended parties. Avoid such conflicts by securing

resonators, and kazooists in case of failure or loss. Leadership qualities include courage, imagination, and—most important—availability. The usual selection method for kazoo band leadership is default.

One word of caution: Beware of overzealous volunteers (petty power mongers, aka PPMs), who seek power and prestige, rather than contributing effort to the general good.

Band Recruitment

Drumming up interest in band membership requires ingenuity and imagination. Overtures to recruits include peer pressure, wheedling, and sometimes, shameless begging. Also effective are promises, bribes, and offers of food or possibly a beverage.

Shanghai sailor tactics (kidnapping) are illegal and

proper permissions and parade permits ahead of time, and keep your group within the bounds of permitted expression.

Another important kazoo-keeping duty is to ensure a ready inventory of spare instruments,

were questionable even when in vogue during the 16th and 17th centuries.

Instant Multiplication:
One way of rapidly increasing your ranks is to issue multiple kazoos to individual members. It is then possible for single kazooists to perform on several kazoos at once, either in tandem or by simultaneous insertion in the mouth cavity of larger-lipped kazooists. This enlarges your total kazooing output up to three or four times normal capacity over that of unikazooists.

Despite the raw musicianship of new recruits, do not be discouraged. Remember that every great artist was first a beginner, although it is the wish of every good leader (and the audience) that some of them progress beyond that.

Think System of Kazooing
(Successmanship)

As in the Broadway show *The Music Man*, any kazooist can magically play if he or she only *believes*—provided there is also a talented librarian to teach the aspirant how to play, while no one else is looking.

The Think System rests somewhere between self-esteem and the outer limits of extreme over-confidence. If you think the tune, you can kazoo it—or at least make some sort of pleasurable noises to accompany your thoughts.[5] (The Think System is also useful for flying, but the only known successful flights have hitherto been by storybook characters such as Peter Pan, who are either animations or mechanically assisted actors.)

[5]The Think System is totally different from the Kamikaze method of performance, which is to play and get bombed.

The secret to thinkmanship is image, image, image—out of earshot of parents, teachers, critics, or anyone who might threaten the process by introducing reality into the situation.

Splendid uniforms for kazoos and kazooists are also an important element in the think technique, disguising those who remain musically challenged by presenting a professional façade. (See also uniforms, below.)

Uniforms

Appropriate attire is always optional. To free-spirited kazooists, "kazoo uniform" is an oxymoron, although many start out dressed alike. Creative

> **Never kazoo tomorrow what you can kazoo today.**

MORE SAFETY CONSIDERATIONS

- Stay clear of areas of potential hostility from nonkazooists (hospital zones, schools in session, sound-triggered mine fields, and so on).

- During rain or lightning storms, wear shoes for outdoor concerts that require using microphones or other electrical equipment.

- Be particularly mindful when taking the rest position in fields or tall weeds where the kazooist and instrument are at heightened risk from trampling or flattening. If you are trespassing, keep your ear to the ground to detect potential stampedes, earthmoving or other farm equipment, or ill-humored property owners.

- Watch for airborn inhalation risks such as flying insects; industrial pollution or smog; excessive perfume in audience; dust devils (whirling dirt storms, especially prevalent in desert areas and in the proximity of household vacuum cleaners); snowballs, dirt clods, and other air-propelled missiles; instrument-barrel blockers (pocket lint); animal fur, feathers, or low-flying bats with damaged radar; chimney soot, airborne pine needles, or other Christmas debris.

costuming is the art of illusion and creates a visage of esprit de corps in an otherwise heterogeneous assemblage. The key is to find a distinctive outfit that identifies all who wear it as members of the group. However, plan ahead to avoid litigation, and expect expensive mandated changes in costuming if you are not politically cautious in your choice.

The uniform T-shirt is always popular. It is affordable and can easily be emblazoned with band names and inspirational mottos or messages. Color coordinating combinations are limitless, although it is recommended that a noncolorblind band member be placed on the selection committee to prevent argumentative response from other members. The egalitarian solution to variance of sizes, shapes, and personal preferences of individual kazooists is unisex sizing—one size that fits no one.

Kazooists are notoriously disorganized, so expect disaster. Bring duct tape, safety pins, and extra outfits. There is inevitably one kazooist who has blue socks instead of black or one part of his/her uniform missing (hopefully not something strategic): plume from hat . . . or gloves . . .

or epaulets. Someone might also fall in a mud puddle getting off the bus and the uniform that ought to be snow white is now more speckled-hen effect. Bring spare parts or trade the band member out to another unit.

Theme Band Costuming:
Inventive costuming is the key to theme bands. For example, Rat Race drill teams wear business suits (or rat costumes) and carry "brellies" (umbrellas) and briefcases; Elvis Impersonators can form entire Elvis bands; Firefighter bands may ride in their own fire truck with Dalmatian-spotted flamingo as hood ornament; Irish Dooley mug look-alikes carry Dooley mugs; Oktoberfest Oom-pah bands dress as tubas; Press Corps wear hats crafted from newspaper; Chocolate Chip

Cookie look-alikes band together; and so on.

Practical Accessorizing:
Depending on budgetary considerations, economy groups often opt for distinctive accessories, such as wigs, hats, or bags, or for hand-held props, such as lawn chairs.

Hats are among the most practical methods to achieve a unifying effect for a minimal

investment. Paper, particularly newspaper, is within most budget constraints, and toy-soldier hats, of the variety made in kindergarten, are easily folded to include appropriate slogans on the brim. However, paper has the disadvantage of limited durability, particularly during rainstorms and in swimming pools. If the paper hat option is exercised, it is important to keep a shower cap or waterproof shopping bag on hand to cover such emergency situations.

Lobster bibs are another popular unifying item, as are garbage bags and plastic or aluminum foil food-wrap modifications, particularly in areas prone to wet weather.

Baseball caps, Sherlock Holmes–style hats, sailor hats, and other cloth hats are among the most practical of operative accessories. They are readily available, can adjust to fit anyone, and are easily embroidered, lettered, or painted. The creative kazooist can easily make alterations appropriate to the occasion. Stuffed animals or objects mounted on top, duck bills, tent flaps, pinwheels, flags, feathers, and other ornamental appurtenances from the outlandish to the lovely—anything is possible from designing minds.

Ribbons, Medals, and Ornamental Sashes:
Always an addition, these can be added with discretion to further disguise the musical effort. Epaulets, cat and dog show ribbons, and other decorative touches can be affixed with great effect. Medals to honor occasions on which the kazooist has been artistically shot down are always appropriate.

Kazoo Couture

Attention should be paid not only to the uniform of the kazooist but also to that of the kazoo, the more ingenious the better. Band names or inspirational slogans can be embossed or stamped on either metal or plastic kazoos. Patriotic flags or other costuming can also easily be attached by rubber band to the kazoo turret.

ARTIST IMPLEMENTS

There are two known public displays of celebrity kazoos:
- *Smithsonian Institution, Washington, D.C.:* By official request, Barbara Stewart's performance kazoo is contained in the collection of the Musical Instruments Department: "one kazoo, blue plastic, inscribed KEEP AMERICA HUMMING." (There was also another one somewhere in a drawer that came by accident on a drum set, but no one knows where it went.)
- *Country Music Hall of Fame and Museum, Nashville, Tennessee:* Kazoo belonging to Jimmie Rodgers, who is known as the "Father of Country Music."

Kazoo Color Coordination

The most popular color combination of historic kazoos was red and blue in the same instrument, although kazoos could be obtained then, as now, in a wide variety of colors. If kazooists think ahead, they can order instruments in almost any solid color or combination for any organization or school, with custom imprinting.

For most kazooists, color choice depends on personal preference or what is handy.

Kazoobas, Zoophoniums, and Like Instruments

Mother is the invention of much great kazooing, and a search through cupboards (with permission) or the instrument junkyard can be very productive. The standard sousaphone was invented by a tuba player from John Philip Sousa's band, who redesigned the instrument to rest its weight on the shoulder and curved the bell to project bass tones forward. (The new bell-forward design also kept out the rain.) With a little imagination, duct tape, and scavenged parts, new brass kazoos can be made from an astonishing variety of parts, as long as the kazooist provides the necessary voice.

Creating New Instruments by Combining Conventional Instruments and Kazoos

The kazoo can effectively be used as a mouthpiece on any standard brass instrument. The tuba with kazoo mouthpiece becomes a kazooba, the baritone horn becomes a zaritorn, the bugle becomes a bazoogle, the trumpet becomes a trumpoo, the French horn becomes a French hornazoo, and so on. The kazoo can also be used as a mouthpiece for certain woodwind instruments, such as clarinet (clarizoo) or saxophone (saxophoo).

Anticipatory Awards

In the spirit of fairness—and to avoid jealousy and greed—awards should be made to each kazooist or music unit before the start of any competition. This ensures uniformly pleasant expression on acceptance. As in Hollywood, complete attention can then be given to who is wearing what and who is seen with whom, leaving inconsequential standards such as talent and musical value out of the equation.

Ideally, a blanket award should be presented to every child at birth, so it is over and done with and the kazooist can get on with real creativity, rather than relentless pursuit of affirmation.

Touring
Travel swiftly and always under cover of darkness.

Marching Along
Importance of Band Names
(Nomenclature)

Even more important than the membership or the musical skill of individual marchers is the acquisition of a distinctive band name. For example, Kazoophony's marching unit is called the Red, White, and Kazoo Band and the Kazoovatory Drum and Bagel Corps. One of the more interesting groups, The 19th Ward Community Association Fully Integrated Affirmative Action Kazoo Marching Band, began in Rochester, New York, in 1974, led by kazoo guru Bob Larter. As they progressed in experience (although not in skill), they added the Electric Drill Team Auxiliary. With an intensive five-minute practice session, they marched without personal injury, playing kazoos and carrying cordless electric drills. No recognizable patterns, formations, or even traditions seem to have resulted.

Practice exercise for a kazoo band (marching or otherwise): Sing the verse to the tune of "Waltzing Matilda." Kazoo on the refrain, to the same tune, using the syllables "doo" and "dee" as indicated.

"Marching Kazilda"
Verse 1
As I was a-walkin'
A-walkin' down that
    country road,
I heard the sound of a
    lonely kazoo.
So I picked up my feet
And I started marchin' to
    the beat;

Then I just joined in that
    doo doo dee doo.

Refrain (kazoo):
Doo-doo dee-doo-doo
Doo-doo dee-doo-doo
Doo doo dee-doo-doo dee-
    doo-doo dee doo
Doo doo doo doo doo doo

**The 39th Street Kazoo Marching
Band and Sis Boom Bah Chorus**

Jerry Darvin

doo dee doo-dee doo doo-
    dee-doo
Doo doo dee-doo-doo dee-
    doo-doo dee doo.

Verse 2
So the two of us was marchin'
A-marchin' down that
    country road;
Up comes another man
A-playin' kazoo.
So he picked up his feet
And he started marchin' to
    that beat;
Then he just joined in the
    doo doo dee doo.

(Refrain)

Verse 3
So we kept on a-marchin'
A-marchin' down that
    country road;
Soon we had joined up a
    whole bloomin' band
    (Ain't it grand).

> **One small note for
> kazooists, one joyous note
> for mankind.**

So we picked up our feet
And we kept on marchin' to
    that beat;
Please wontcha join us in
    doo doo dee doo.

(Refrain)

*(At end, fade out on last line of
"dees" and "doos.")*

Marching Chants and Verbal Count-offs

For professional appearance, use
rhythmic counts and chants to
disguise imprecision in actual
drill. Rhyming, however nonsen-
sical, can also serve the same
function. For example, without
a real tune, you can chant lyrics
such as:

Count off, 1-2 (Pause) 3-4
We are march-ing and
    kazoo-ing;
We don't know what we are
    do-ing . . .

Most Basic of Marching Techniques

1. Make certain the field is clear of attack animals, players, or other hazards.

2. Remember to guide right (look to your right, to make sure you are properly lined up with the others in your row), except when you are turning left. In the latter case, guide left.

3. To avoid unpleasant confrontation, do not step on other band members.

To start, on the count of "one," conventional bands step onto the LEFT foot. Ordinarily the left foot comes down on the strong beat, except when kazooists choose to switch feet for amusing effect.

WHAT TO BRING TO BAND CAMP OR OTHER KAZOO EXCURSIONS

- Kazoo with necklace, so you can locate your instrument
- Chapstick
- Kazoo name tag
- Tape to keep teeth from chipping (for marching and no-handed kazooing)

Collateral Duty (Nonkazooing): Marching Band Job Descriptions

Many important nonkazooing marching band positions are available for the unitone or arbitrary-pitch kazooist. These auxiliary band positions for the musically challenged can add immeasurably to the depths of everyone's enjoyment. Participants such as Flag Flippers, Foof-Foof Squads (named for the sound their pom-poms make), and Baton Droppers (who randomly throw batons in the air) can finally be given their rightful place at the forefront.

Banner Bearers: Participants of varying heights make the task of carrying a banner infinitely more difficult, requiring strategic placement of shorter people in the center and taller ones on each end. The more similar the height of Banner Bearers, the more likely the banner is to stay straight—and the less argument about who stands where.

Fitness also plays an important part, since a tired Banner Bearer may cause a banner to droop, presenting potential hazards of ripping and tripping.

Baton Droppers: Twirlers who lack dexterity cannot fail in this assignment, although care should be exercised to avoid injury to yourself or your marching unit. The baton is hurled into the air with no attempt whatsoever to retrieve it before it drops and bounces one or more times on the ground.

> **There's safety in numbers: Join a band.**

Flag Flippers: Former cheerleaders and bugle-corps color guards make excellent recruits for this opening. They usually march with the Baton Droppers at the head of the parade so flags don't get tangled up with the kazooists. Auxiliary (nonkazooist) marchers may use a variety of custom-designed flag poles and flags, letting imagination and taste guide selection. A favorite is a regular-size flag pole with an extremely tiny flag, in keeping with the scale of the kazoo.

Colorless Guards: A variation of the Flag Flippers is a line of marchers carrying a white flag of surrender to ensure safety, in case they get going in the direction of a hostile crowd.

Foof-Foof Squads (Pom-Pom Girls): Not to be forgotten are the Pom-Pom Girls, who may be of any gender, as specified by the band director. They are technically referred to as the "Foof-Foof

Squad," so named for the sound their colorful pom-poms make in combined motion ("foof-foof"). They add much to the festive appearance of marching bands, providing nonmusical roles for those who wish to participate in decorative and rhythmic functions rather than add any musicality.

On a purely practical level, Foof-Foof Squads are especially recommended for tropical environments, where pom-pom motion can provide fan functionality to aid in air circulation.

Canine Corps and Other Pet Patrols: Some pets might be capable of kazooing if properly trained. Experts are certain that pigs could accomplish kazooing if they could be persuaded to play them before they ate them. To date, this has not been successfully demonstrated, so animals generally march as nonkazooing auxiliaries.

Dogs are particularly useful as guards to protect the rear flanks from other marching units such as llamas and motorcycle units. They may also be fitted with collar kegs to supply thirsty kazooists with liquid sustenance during long parades.

Note: Although llamas do not kazoo, they do hum when agitated.

Spray Spritzer Operators: Auxiliary marchers carrying clean plant spray bottles or automatic (repeating) water pistols can revive parch-lipped kazooists during the parade. Spray Spritzer Operators can also act as guides for the marching-unit columns and call out instructions, count off, and so on. This is easy for them to do, since they will not be talking with their mouths full, as will performing kazooists.

LLAMA CAUTIONARY

When kazooing around llamas, use extreme caution.[6] Llamas and alpacas are notoriously ambivalent in their feelings for kazooists, since normal communication of alarm in llama language is a remarkably kazoolike humming sound. They also spit.

The importance of this was demonstrated at the Hudson Wisconsin Hot Air Affair Ballooning Festival and Kazoo Band Parade, where llamas were uncertain whether they were more afraid of the kazooists or the "phooming" fiery outbursts from the propane heaters for the balloons.

Llamas indicate an uneasiness that necessitates rearranging their parade position to place them at the head of the parade rather than to the rear of the kazoo bands. This way, if inclined to stampede, llamas run forward toward someone else rather than trampling kazooists behind them.

[6]This caution refers to the animal-kingdom llama, not religious leaders (lamas) from Tibet. As Ogden Nash explains it, "One-L lama, he's a priest; two-L llama, he's a beast."

THE "RUN ON" TECHNIQUE

If kazooists are musically marginal, a good show may consist of a rapid "run on," usually from an end zone, with the band dashing to opening position. This might be followed with a fast-moving drill (dissolve and scatter tactics), so no one can judge precision. Then play something short, with band stationary or moving slightly (listing or accidentally swaying can be mistaken for planned action, so don't worry about this among the unsteady band members). Another quick tune and a complicated drill at the end, double-timed for rapid exit, can create the illusion of more skill than was actually mustered.

Repercussionists: Although pitch can be arbitrary, it is always desirable to have rhythm or beat in a parade. A real drummer is an excellent addition, but if this is not an option, kitchen percussion (spoon/pan units), laundry units (washtub/washboard combos), and other adaptations are acceptable.

Electronic Enhancers (Surround Sound): Technicians

with electronic enhancement devices can assist greatly by adding recorded kazoo music as backup to aid the live band's efforts. Expert musicians providing background sound with bullhorns, speakers, and microphones or recorded beat can all greatly improve the morale (and musical output) of the marching unit. Kazooists can then relax and lip synch, which is much easier for hummers than trying to match word articulation.

Human Mascots: Mascots are the symbolic representatives of your outfit, so choose wisely. For example, former hockey, football, and basketball players are often agile, but may be aggressively preconditioned and enter into unexpected combat with rival mascots. Cheerleaders, mimes, actors, and dancers are safer.

Kazoo Majors and Minors for Parade Leadership: It is desirable to recruit at least one member with the ability to lead a marching unit, preferably one who can count. Tall is good also, since the Kazoo Major by

AVANT-GARDE CANADIAN KAZOO BAND MAKES NEW NOISE

The Nihilist Spasm Band from London, Ontario—the oldest continuously operating noise band around—has been mixing kazoos and disorganized sound, e.g., homemade and plugged-in instruments, since the 1960s. They are skilled musicians who systematically dismantle sound and experiment with electronic kazooing, remaining one of the foremost musicless bands.

definition is in the lead and needs to be highly visible to followers. If the Kazoo Major lacks sufficient stature, increased elevation can be gained with assistive devices such as a tall hat and high-heeled sneakers.

Motorized Units

Motorized units work best when participants are old enough to drive, but those without licenses can invent their own transportation methods. There is no limit to the creative imagination of the young, although most schools have plenty of authorities to make certain it does not exceed the bounds of their perception of good taste. Tricycles, shopping carts, skateboards, skis (in colder climates), and other assistive devices have all been tried with success.

Increasing the Number of Bands in a Parade

To create the illusion of more bands participating, the easiest way is to place your band at the front of the parade. After reaching the reviewing stand or parade ending point, execute scramble formation to reform at the end of the parade, beginning again as a second unit. If your members are fast enough, this can be done multiple times.

Beefing Up Bands:
Another solution is to intersperse trucks with speakers blaring recorded kazoo music, employing lip-synching recruits. Participants can usually be commandeered from spectators or bandless marching units such as Girl and Boy Scouts, Little Leaguers, and so on. Playing along rather than silently lip-synching enhances the depth of the experience, rather than ruining the music, since kazooist music is fuzzy anyway.

Scripted Performance:
For professional appearance, use an announcer reading from a script to make the show as dramatic as possible. Review the script beforehand to make certain it is appropriate and will not elicit disciplinary action from school or other officials.

Repercussion:

In regular corps-style bands, in addition to marching drummers and percussion, use a "drum pit" on the field, where percussion players with larger instruments, such as marimbas, xylophones, drum sets, tympani, gongs, etc. reside. Kazoo bands may use toy or homemade percussion instruments. One of the most popular is maracas made out of plastic soda bottles and filled with fishing weights or BBs to create homemade rattles.

Precision Marching Formations

All formations are funnier—and more difficult—if done in close-order drill with band members standing shoulder to shoulder.

General Advice:

Like sports teams, kazoo bands have both offensive and defensive strategies. The element of surprise is important, as are bluffing and overwhelming the opposition with numbers.

Kazooists use standard commands, such as "to the rear, march," "about face," "mark time," "parade rest," "halt," "at ease," "kazoos up," and so on. In addition, creative choreography can add hops, skips, face-offs, zigzags, and dance steps of every variety. This requires careful diagramming, adaptation to conditions, and a *lot* of practice.

Slide Step Maneuver to Begin Songs:

1. In left direction, take 4 slide steps sideways, counting out loud to take each step, 1-2-3-4. (On the count of ONE, stand on your RIGHT foot and take a large sidestep with your

COOL BAND MOVES THAT ARE EASY

Kazoo University Salute: Count out loud as you step left-right (one-two). Holding kazoo in left hand, raise arm straight above head and chant "Kazoo U!" Drop arm and repeat sequence as often as desired.

Kazoo Cheer: Kazooing on the lowest possible pitch performed in long, drawn-out monotone, repeat each letter in Kazoo Banding as follows:

K is for the K in Ka-zoo Band-ing
A is for the A in Ka-zoo Band-ing
Z is for the Z in Ka-zoo Band-ing
O is for the O in Ka-zoo Band-ing
O is for the O in Ka-zoo Band-ing
. . .
Continue on to spell "banding," and keep going until you are all spelled out.

LEFT foot. Move your RIGHT foot in a sliding motion to meet your left foot. Do the same for "Two," "Three," and "Four.")

2. Yell "Halt!" and STOP where you are.

3. Yell "Ready!"

4. On count of "One," take a LEFT STEP IN PLACE.

5. On "Two," do a RIGHT KICK FORWARD. (Kick right foot out in front—not into another kazooist.)

6. On "Three," SWING SAME LEG (right) BACK.

7. On "Four," STEP DOWN on RIGHT foot. (Remember to execute this last step or right foot will remain in the air throughout.)

8. Yell "Play!" and start the music.

In-Place Front Slide (Treadmill Step):
A remarkably simple move that looks great is a Gene Kelly creation. The kazooist bends forward at the waist, swinging arms up and down in exaggerated sprinter's arm motions to balance, while he/she takes repeated large frontward sliding steps in place, as if on a treadmill.

This looks really professional, but does not actually get you anywhere, since you end up exactly where you started (hence

descriptive name "in-place slide"). Choose another technique to get from one place to another.

Swing Shift Kazooing:
In regular bands, saxophones, trumpets, trombones, sousaphones, and the like often swing their instruments in time to the music.

For kazoo coordination, synchronize swinging left to right. If you have a large or bulky kazoo, such as a tromboo, bazoogle, kazooba, or other handcrafted mutation, be careful not to take out your neighbor, especially when making turns or sudden halts.

Kazoos to the Box:
A particularly impressive maneuver for regular marching bands is called "horns to the box," where bands point their instruments, flags, and whatever at the press box in salute.

Kazoo bands have a similar move, but since instruments are smaller, flags also need to be smaller to adapt to scale.

We shall overhum!

Northern Wisconsin
"Hudson Huddle":
Close-order drill formation is obviously the most expeditious for northerly kazooing. It keeps troops warm. It has the additional advantage of disguising whatever is going on in the middle, so there is no way anyone can tell what the participants

are doing, much less whether or not they're doing it correctly. It does leave outer edges exposed, so it is important to encircle neophytes with more experienced marchers.

Sideways Columns:
Marching sideways is one of the more hazardous moves, since an abrupt column movement marching either right or left could startle curbside onlookers, causing them to view this as a

hostile move in their direction. That could result in counter-attack on their part, with the possibility of bodily harm for band members. If this does happen, the Retreat or Exit Scatter formation should immediately follow as a countermove. The about face is *not* recommended in this situation, since this could cause the same problem on the opposite side of the street and hostile crowds would then be attacking from both sides.

Spiral:
In this exercise, the band moves single file in a circular pattern, winding either clockwise or counterclockwise into the center. This is rarely accomplished successfully, since one or more kazooists are invariably listening to the beat of a different drummer and wind counter-

clockwise when the others are winding clockwise, creating a traffic jam and jeopardy to all.

"Retrogression" or "Backward" Technique:
Kazoo bands often march backward, but very carefully and *never* in cow pastures.

Mergers and Acquisitions:
As is often the case with volunteer organizations, kazoo band members tend to drop in and out without prior warning. The skillful director takes advantage of this natural occurrence, tightening and expanding the ranks to adapt as part of the choreography. In order to significantly increase numbers, it is sometimes possible to absorb entire rival bands, either by persuasion or simply by close-order marching to infiltrate their ranks.

Slide Step:
This may be used in any region, but is easy in northern icy climates. It is also well adapted to the smooth gymnasium floor environment. For a left slide step, step to the left on the left foot, then bring the right foot even with the left in a gliding motion. It may be expeditious to label shoes ("right" and "left") to avoid any directional ambiguity.

Letter Formations:
Since many kazooists turn to kazooing because they don't know the words, spelling may be equally troublesome. Also, kazoo bands often lack sufficient numbers to spell out whole words (or even a complete letter). Consider supplementing with banners or signs if you really must spell something.

Bombshell Scatter:
A classic transition to new formation is to first clump together and then scatter (run) individually to your next position. As long as you all end up somewhere appropriate this is effective, but it may be confusing if not everyone can be accounted for after the scatter. Appoint a spotter to locate strays, if necessary.

"Retreat" or
"Exit Scatter" Formation:
This is basically a "head for the hills" countermovement and may constitute the final motion in a series of preceding and unsuccessful countermoves. Saving face is distinctly the better part of valor for kazooists, with personal safety always a primary priority.

Corps-Style Marching Bands:
Precision marching bands are always fashionable, but a preferred new look is "Corps Style," which incorporates constant motion and evolution of patterns during the musical number. This is entirely suited to kazooists, who generally lean more toward free form than strict adhesion to precision and perhaps might not recognize the latter if they ran into it. Corps Style has the advantage of making it difficult to judge what the band meant to do in the first place, once they are already in the process of moving ahead to do something else.

Corps-Style groups do designs of all kinds on the field—though no "picture shows" or spelling as seen in Big Ten or Ivy League shows. These designs are abstract and supposedly reflect the style of the music. The bands often appear to be wandering around, lost, aimlessly searching for something or other. They march sideways and backward a lot, with the bells of their horns pointing at the stands.

Advanced Marching:
Asymmetric formations are far more practical than symmetric ones, since audiences have no preconceived notion of what was intended and so tend to be less critical.

Special attention should be paid to the following moves: crossovers, pass-throughs, and pass-outs; cut-and-paste transitions; division and remainders (goes-intos and leftovers); impact and other unfortunate transitions; floating blocks, pods, and washouts; rotations and over-expansions; guarded motions and arrest.

Optical Illusions

Advanced Band Formations:
When the mind processes visual images, humans are able to compensate for missing information and effects such as distortion in perspective or trick effects. Thus, it is possible to construct images (optical illusions) that mislead the brain, causing two-dimensional information to be "seen" as a three-dimensional image. This concept is particularly useful for kazoo bands, which often require the illusion of having more members than they are able to recruit.

The optimal vantage point for audiences to view Optical Illusion formations is from airplanes or blimps over the field. This greatly enhances the effect,

generally better from far away. It also increases the element of personal safety for kazooists, in case audiences are displeased with their efforts.

Horizontal Lines Parallel or Slippery Slope Formation: Individual, follow-the-leader columns (five Kazooists in each) space themselves apart from each other at intervals of 3 to 6 feet, in a herringbone pattern, as shown below. Kazoo columns make parallel intersections at diagonal angles to the parallel field markings. This will appear to be sloped or ragged lines— even though the field markings remain stationary. This makes perfect sense to kazooists, whose lines are often a bit fuzzy to

begin with and who understand
that everything is relative and
the earth moves anyway, even if
the band stands still.

Tall / Short Effects:
Experiment with placement of
different-size kazooists, placing
some very tall people around a
small-size person, making that
central person look shorter than
in a group of very short people.
If you don't have the right size
personnel, stand on boxes for
tallness and sit for shortness.

Field Marking Illusions:
Bent or converging lines drawn
on the field will also create
unique illusions when kazooists
march over them.

*All in the Eye of the Beholder
Formation (Perspective Illusions):*
Vary distances between people.
The closer to the audience, the
closer band members should be
to each other—or vice versa.
Watch out for unwanted frater-
nization on the close-order drill
side of the band.

Made in the Shade Formation:
Use lighting effects to change
the colors of uniforms, placing
some band members in the
"shade" and some others in the
"light," making the color of their
uniforms look the same,
although they are different (or
the other way round). Change
positions for a contrasting effect.

3-D Delusions:
Issue 3-D eyeglasses to the
audience to create the illusion
of three-dimensional effect. The

eyeglasses will do nothing for them visually unless they are viewing a moving picture created in 3-D technology, but with a little imagination the audience may be convinced they are part of something mysterious and wonderful.

Pinwheels:
Line up eight (more or less) kazooists to form the spokes of a pinwheel. One kazooist anchors (does not move), and kazooists at the apex (center) move slower than those at the outer end, so lines whirl around as units. Center kazooists should not start too fast; if they do, lonely end kazooists may whip out of control and end up splattered into fences or viewing stands.

Also keep your distance from other spokes (lines of kazooists), so you don't cause pileups, which is another formation altogether.

Photo Op Formation:
Like sports teams, Kazoo bands must always be prepared for Photo Opportunities, so the clever kazoo band thinks ahead by marching in this formation.

Kazooists in the front crouch, middle line marches in semi-standing position, and kazooists in the rear, standing-up-straight line place crossed kazoos behind the heads of the line ahead, like small children placing devil's horns behind classmates to ruin the photo.

If All Else Fails Formation: March on, take several bows—encouraging applause—and leave before the audience realizes you haven't done anything yet.

Specialty Bands

Pep Bands

Pep bands are groups of kazooists recruited by schools or other organizations to show up and embarrass themselves. Kazooing offers the great advantage of eliminating any necessity to memorize words of school or other theme songs, since the

natural buzzing bombardment of the instrument obfuscates any momentary mind-blips.

Chanting and kazooing are a natural combination for marching (see page 102) or stand bands (at right), either simultaneously or in alternation. For football, kickoff chants include stadium-side volleys, in which one side of the stadium yells something unintelligible and the other side yells something else in reply.

The primeval aspects intrinsic to the competitive spirit can be greatly heightened by kazooing. However, be sure you are kazooing in the zone approved for your loyalties, staying clear of enemy turf.

> **K-a-z-o-o, c'mon, kazoo, kazoo, let's go!**

Fan Band in the Stands

Sports events and other exhibitions of legalized violence offer perfect opportunities for exuberant kazooing, either extemporaneously or in rehearsed effort. There is safety in numbers, so band together with others of similar interest in the stands.

Professional sports and music markets are inextricably bonded in commercial interests, so stadium music is often blasted on speakers to excite fans and stimulate sales. Kazoo bands can add greatly to the pummeling aspects of pop-drenched, fist-waving fight music.

We Will, We Will Rock You: The #1 stadium fight song is "We Will Rock You," by Queen. Kazoo fan bands require only a simplistic excerpt, substituting "doo doo, doo doo, doo-doo" for

WE WILL, WE WILL ROCK YOU

MUSIC SEGMENT (kazooed)

F	E	D	C	D	D
Doo	Doo,	Doo	Doo	Doo -	Doo!

LAP-SLAP AND CLAP SECTION

Lap-slap, lap-slap, clap;
Lap-slap, lap-slap, clap;
Lap-slap, lap-slap, clap.

(Continued in endless repetitions, stopping when you feel like it.)

F	E	D	C	D	D
Doo	Doo,	Doo	Doo	Doo -	Doo!

(And so on. . . .)

words. Each six-note segment consists of four descending pitches (one of which is used three times) followed by a lap-slap and clap section, which continues in endless repetitions. (It is also acceptable to substitute foot stomps for lap slaps.) Fans sometimes erroneously execute the wrong numbers of lap slaps and claps, probably because they have this mixed up with "The Hey Song" (see below). Kazooists are not bothered by this, as long as it is noisy and fun.

Hey Song:
Another hit sporting-event anthem is popularly known as "The Hey Song" ("Rock and Roll, Part Two").

WHOO-WHOO HEY SONG

SING

      F   E   D   C

      Whoo whoo whoo whoo (repeat)

      F   G   A

      Who-oo Who-oo Who-oo-oo

(Hold and drop last "oo" in descending-pitch bent tone)

SHOUT

      "Hey!"

UNDULATING DRUM BREAK

      Da-lop-pada, lop-pada, lop-pada lop

CHANT

      Play kazoo!

This one has three pitches (descending F-E-D), kazooed with never-ending repetitions of "naa, naa, naa," followed by the shouted lyric "Hey!" in between overamplified rhythmic riffs.

The kazooless (purely vocal) version often just goes "dada-dada-dah-dah-HEY!" ad infinitum to pump up interest by primordial heartbeat simulation. ("Thumpa-thumpa-thump-thump-HEY!" would be more direct and easier to remember but requires advanced mastery of diction.)

Whoo-Whoo Hey Song
This not-yet-hit new song by Kazoophony fits directly into the genre, reusing notes in infinite repetition, employing monosyllabic lyrics and simplistic percussive effects.

Red Hat Society Bands

In keeping with a tradition of silliness, red hats, purple outfits, and free-form fun, the Red Hat Society designates the kazoo as its official instrument.

Invention is for all you mothers of necessity, so put forth your best creative skills. Here is one possibility to get you started. Start in scramble, running (or wheeling) to the middle to form a human bonnet. Arrange yourselves according to color, standing at attention in your assigned grid position to begin. Start with a clipped military fanfare, such as "Do de da doot da dooo!"

Choreograph dance moves to "In Your Easter Bonnet,"

undulating and swirling to change positions and perhaps form a different hat. Busby Berkeley– and Ziegfeld Folly– style showgirl moves are admirably suited to this.

One easy move is the Drag and Step, as if you were in a wedding. This is particularly effective when accompanied by exaggerated postures and modeling moves.

Golden Age Bands

Senior citizens bands have the advantage of recruiting seasoned performers. In addition, the instrument is intrinsically suited to older-voice vocalization. The rasping edge and the bombardment of sound allow the mature voice to sound no better or worse than any other age voice, demonstrating the marvelous equalizing quality of kazooing.

The kazoo is indeed the most democratic of instruments—the "great leveler." In fact, a cracking older voice may enhance the complex antagonistic overtones that create the remarkable fuzziness of kazoo timbre.

Golden age bands often add kitchen instruments, such as musical spoons or percussive saucepans. This has the particular advantage of having them handy for rehearsal snacks, a valuable incentive in recruiting new members and keeping the active ones active.

Many mature bands also choose to get in tune with youth, teaching children and kazooing in harmonious amalgamation across the generations. At live-in facilities, instruments should be labeled and, if necessary, confiscated at the end of rehearsal or performance.

AP/Wide World Photos

The kazoo is especially popular with more mature musicians.

When senior citizens or the physically handicapped take to the streets for parade duty, the recommended formation is motorized units. Golf carts, decorated band buses, and hay wagons are among favored modes of transportation. Individual motorized wheelchairs or attendant-piloted wheelchair squadrons should exercise the utmost caution and make certain proper distance is kept in order to avoid collisions.

Genre Bands: Pop Culture and Commercial Kazooing

Many critics claim that pop culture produces music by the talentless for the tasteless. Kazooists can embrace this highly attainable goal, as well as the potential for excessive monetary reward.

Of the 107 categories offered for 30 genres of music in the Grammy Awards, not one is offered for Kazoo Music. For kazooists there is simply nowhere to go but up.

Pop culture and commercial venues actually offer more categories of music than there are varieties of music: hard, soft, and rolling rock; heavy or other metallurgical forms; mine rock (musical newscasting); rhythm and kazoos; urban/alternative; suburban-garage style; rap, crackle, and Latin pop; gospel; country; folkabilly; Texmex; electronic; unplugged; unleashed; and so on.[7] There are not really that many differences, just different names and much overlapping (fuzzy boundaries). If your genre

[7]There is also R & B (rhythm and blues), although R & V (recreation and vehicles) is even more popular among kazooists.

> **Many are called, but kazoos are chosen.**

is unclear, make up a category and pretend it's something new. Where the old stops and new stuff comes in is in the ears of the beholder. Let the profits begin.

Some mainstream music celebrities depend on an audience whose perception may be altered by pharmaceuticals or possibly a beverage or two, so it matters little what goes on in the music. This should NOT be the approach for the dedicated kazooist, since at best those are anesthetized responses and at the other end of the spectrum may even incite violence. This could lead to incarceration, legal fees, and even confiscation of your instrument. Although celebrity artists have highly paid attorneys (who list their address as a major airline, shuttling between indictments of clients), this is not the way for budget-conscious kazoo artists to live. Rather, the kazooist should find new ways to attract and entertain the audience.

Pop Divas

Musicality is irrelevant to attaining pop diva status, which pop dictionaries define simply as "goddess" (not to be confused with opera divas, who have glorious voices and—like pop divas—attitude and a powerful agent). To attain Kazoo Pop Diva status, follow the spirit of other deities and hurricanes and use a single name. (Cher, Björk, Beyoncé, Barbra, Madonna, Britney, and Celine are already taken.)

kazooists, are irrelevant. Try "Whoo whoo, play kazoo . . ." or some such utterance.

Rap

Choose an appropriate name such as Kazoop Doggy Dawg or whatever. Luckily diction is irrelevant to rap, so kazooing will have little or no effect on obscuring your already incomprehensible message. The important thing is to sound angry, even if you're not.

The kazoo is also admirably adapted because there are so many words that rhyme with kazoo, making it possible for even the least articulate to find something they can work with.

Examples of kazoo rap words to select from are: kazoo, you, true, new, stew, few, doo, through, brew, queue, goo, hue, zoo, eeuu, mew, pew, too, undo, view, wee-

The Big Song for Little Attention Span is important, although content (and certainly lyrics) pale in comparison to the image, staging, and attitude required. Use repetitive phrases, choreographed undulating motion, and lots of free-form noises. Lyrics, particularly for

oouu. Also: hum, bum, rum, numb, dumb, rum tum tum, some, come, thumb, gum, mum, rum pum pum, yum, and Yum-Yum.

Keep your audience busy. Instead of allowing the audience to remain sedentary and unoccupied, to distract from violent response the kazooist should encourage them to jump rope. This hands-full approach occupies their fists, making open

assault on the kazooist beyond their immediate capability.

By tradition, regular jump ropists chant with the rhythm of their words as they execute jumps. However, simultaneous

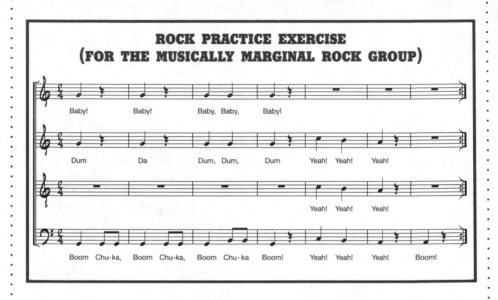

**ROCK PRACTICE EXERCISE
(FOR THE MUSICALLY MARGINAL ROCK GROUP)**

Baby! Baby! Baby, Baby, Baby!

Dum Da Dum, Dum, Dum Yeah! Yeah! Yeah!

Yeah! Yeah! Yeah!

Boom Chu-ka, Boom Chu-ka, Boom Chu-ka Boom! Yeah! Yeah! Yeah! Boom!

jump roping and kazoo chanting is not recommended for the artist due to safety concerns. Leave the jump roping to the audience.

Rock and Metallurgical Forms

Most rock-music forms are characterized by high amplification, driving rhythms, and distorted sound, all perfectly suited to either electrified or unplugged kazooing. Exaggerated lyrics are customarily indecipherable, especially when kazooed through exotic lighting effects and high-volume activity, which are designed to infuse vacuous content with the appearance of somethingness.

Hard, soft, classic, freak, geek, funky, metal, cover bands, multistyle, psychedelic, extro, etro, retro, progressive, heavy metal, rolling, space, and moon rock are all related, except the last two, which are sometimes interplanetary and from NASA rather than musical.

The kazooist who is into '50s-style rock 'n' roll, folk rock, hard rock, disco, punk, or new wave will be pleased to note that the kazoo adapts easily to any of these styles.

The most famous rock kazooist might be Richard Starkey, although he did not kazoo much

> **A kazoo in time saves nine.**

until after he changed his name to Ringo Starr. "You're Sixteen" was a number one hit for Ringo in 1974, but the featured kazooist was Paul McCartney, so Ringo's kazoo artistry appears lost to posterity. Rock groups such as The Lovin' Spoonful and Brooklyn Bridge also kazooed on occasion. None of these groups is still in existence, but the kazoo was probably not instrumental in their breakup.

Jazz Kazooing

Kazooing has played a part in jazz since the beginning. In fact, following the kazoo's American invention in the 1840s—long before jazz was born—kazoos were used in country string bands and every other sort of group imaginable. In generations without microphones, kazoos were affordable by all and used to amplify voices to be heard over the guitars, banjos, and other stringed instruments. Kazoos were everywhere in the evolution of blues and jazz in all forms. Certainly Louie Armstrong's rasping tones could be compared to kazoo resonance, and may have been an imitation of it.

Rasping, sliding, glissing, shifting rhythms, and flattening tones are all techniques used to add interest. Nearly anything can be made jazzy by applying these skills.

Jazz Techniques:
Jazz requires improvising around a melody, leading some critics to refer to jazz as "musical doodling." If you are musical, probably the best approach to jazz is to listen carefully to good performers and imitate their

styles. Learning scat singing is an excellent approach to acquiring good jazz kazoo technique.

If you are not musical, play with loud backup recordings. Softly play along, making an attempt to blend in the least offensive manner.

Written music for jazz looks like other music, except you refer to it as "charts," not "scores." If you can't read music, try wearing sunglasses (shades) during performances. You will not be able to see well, but at least you will look right for the part.

One simple blues technique for the amateur to practice is bending notes. Basically, go for the note, miss it by hitting underneath it, and then slide back to get it. This creates a sort of swooping effect that is readily recognizable in jazz circles. Simple tunes, such as "I've Been Working on the Railroad," can be made to sound much more interesting by using this technique. The expert may wish to go on to adapt Gershwin into *Rhapsody in Kazoo,* using note bending with spectacular effect in the opening clarinet solo. "When the Saints Go Marching In" and "In the

Mood" are two other good jazz practice tunes.

Dixieland is also highly adaptable, especially if you combine the kazoo with a banjo and a tuba, or kazooba (tuba with kazoo mouthpiece) with a

Harmonica legend Hammie Nixon also played a mean kazoo.

trombone and a piano. This type of jazz requires some creative improvisation from the proficient player. It may also be kazooed at its more basic level, by simply humming the melody line of such classics as "Has Anybody Seen My Gal?" which offers innumerable opportunities to rhyme lines with "kazoo" ("blue," "two," and so on).

Plain Folk Kazooing

Among scholars, folk music is traditionally referred to as "the uncouth vocal utterance of the people." Among kazooists, it is known as "fun." It also has the great advantage of invariably falling within one octave of vocal range, which makes it not only fun but possible.

From early periods in villages, on through coffeehouses and taverns, folk has always

been a favorite, particularly among the more fortunate. The message may be an unfathomable expression of something or other, such as "hey-nonnie-nonnie" or "fa-la-la," the meaning of which is lost to antiquity. Generally, it is storytelling, which among genuine peasants often has a depressing message, unless dancing and celebratory beverages are involved to raise spirits.

Noncommercial Messages:
Let us not forget Stephen Foster, gifted songwriter of the 19th century, who swam upstream against public tides to humanize the plight of slaves. Foster was a financial disaster but composed his own tunes and lyrics, which are eminently kazooable and—without words—even politically correctable. "Oh Susannah!" was an all-time hit, for which Foster was paid the handsome sum of extra copies of the sheet music.[8]

Ready, Aim, Sing:
The "folksong army" memorialized by satirist Tom Lehrer reached its zenith in the 1960s–70s, when commercial music discovered the enormously profitable combination of peace, love, weed, and political seed. Even better, folk kazooing minimized the need to write lyrics on hands or cuffs.

There were two major divisions of commercial folkies, most of whom did not discover the advantages of kazooing:

1. Upscale Hopey (optimistic) like Pete Seeger; Peter, Paul and Mary; and The Kingston Trio.

2. Downright Mopey (despairing and dismal) like Bob Dylan and Joan Baez. Affluent singers told downtrodden worker–war stories, all the while keeping a thick upper lip. This apparently caused them to slur words and droop

[8]Stephen Foster's family wanted him to be an accountant, but in classical tradition he stayed faithful to his music and died at age 38 instead.

their eyelids, fitting dums and doos into drowsy extended syllables such as "dooooin's."

Folk-a-Billy Banding:
Rock-music forms are not necessarily new, but simply coin a different name for their genre. Folk kazooists can also do this.

Folk-a-Billy combines the best of folk and real down-home country with a lot of clapping, stomping, and everything up to and including bands without music and kitchen bands with or without a kitchen sink. Folk-a-Billy groups go for the gold but so far haven't even found the silver lining, much less the platinum record, the green stuff, or the brass ring.

"Hummin' in the Wind"
Folk Practice Tune:
> *Verse 1*
> Hum, hum-hum, hum
> Hum, hum, hum, hum.
> Hum-hum, hum-hum,
> Hum-hum, hum?
> Yes'n'
> Hum, hum-hum, hum
> Hum, hum, hum, hum.
> Hum-hum, hum-hum,
> Hum-hum, hum?

Yes'n'
Hum, hum-hum, hum
Hum, hum, hum, hum.
Hum-hum, hum-hum,
Hum-hum, hum?

Chorus
Hum, hum, hum, hum, hum.
Hum, hummin', hum, hum,
   hum.
Hum, hum, hum,
Hum, hummin',
Hum, hum,
Hum.

Celtic Kazooing

No one is sure who the Celts
were, so this is equally unimpor-
tant to Celtic kazooists. Ancient
Celts are described as oddly
dressed barbaric people, with
strange beliefs that resulted in
continuous feuds. Taller than
Romans, Greeks, or Gauls and
generally fair haired, they were

> **Speak little, kazoo much.**

visible everywhere in Europe
and only assigned to the British
Isles by short-sighted historians
of recent centuries. Celts are
probably just misplaced Vikings
who wandered off into frigid
fringe territories, where they
started weaving plaids, dancing,
and making music to keep warm
during rest periods from con-
quering and pillaging.

In modern times, most people
can't tell the difference between
Scottish and Irish kazooing, so
don't worry about differences. To
prevent chipped teeth or other
injuries in any style, if you
dance and also kazoo, do this
alternately, not simultaneously.
Remember that prior to Michael
Flatley's *Lord of the Dance*,

classic Irish dancers kept their arms at their sides. Scottish dancers do not.

Scottish Kazooists:
While Scottish clansmen traditionally store weapons (dirks or knives) in their kneesocks, kazooists are already considered armed and dangerous, so this is unnecessary. However, kneesocks are a handy place to stash your kazoo.

To imitate the bagpipe sound, you need two kazooists—one to produce the "duh-wang, duh-wang" droning sound and the other the tune. It is unnecessary to play in the same key, since the charm of bagpipes is the nasal clash of pitches.

Popular tunes without need for unprounceable Gaelic words are "Did You Ever See a Lassie?," "Charlie Is My Darlin',"

and "Amazing Grace." Kazooing also eliminates the need to understand the meaning of poet Robert Burns's song, "Auld Lang Syne" (see page 178), which is universally celebratory for the New Year, as long as you don't care what it means.

Most bagpipe tunes are in mixolydian mode (medieval form of major scale, with the 7th note a semitone flat). Kazooists do not need the massive air pressure required for actual bagpiping, but should throw caution to the winds to enhance the savage skirling appeal of the music.

Irish Kazooing:
Every St. Patrick's Day in New York, up to 2 million people (nearly half the population of Ireland) take to the streets to overcelebrate, an action that can be amplified by kazooists of any nationality.

Although traditional lyrics are often about terrible tragedies ("Danny Boy," "Kathleen Mavoureen," etc.), kazooists can eliminate sadness by concentrating on melody, playing happy-time songs such as jigs and reels

("Irish Washerwoman"). Kazooists of mixed ethnic heritage can happily combine cultures by adding Hispanic rhythms ("Spanish Washerwoman") or assembling their own songs from multiple nationalities ("Roll Out the Barrel in the Foggy Dew, My Darling Lucia Maria Bublichki").

Country Kazooing

Country music, whether contemporary or "old-timey," tells a story, poses philosophical questions ("Does Your Chewing Gum Lose Its Flavor on the Bedpost Overnight?"), or expresses emotional quandary. It combines bluegrass, poetry, love, hate, abandonment, gospel, cowboy songs, honky-tonk, barrelhouse, and whatever. These are all easily blended into kazoo tonality.

The sound and lyrics for country and western music are generated well up into the nose. Famous country kazooists include Jimmie Rodgers, Gene Autry, and numerous jug- and washboard-band people who recorded in the 1920s and '30s. Also not to be forgotten are Belly Joe and Jelly Dough Kaminsky of Kazoophony's[9] Kaminsky Country Singers.

In addition to bands composed entirely of kazoos, there

[9]For more on Kazoophony, see page 189.

DO-IT-YOURSELF OLD-TIMEY COUNTRY KAZOO PRACTICE TUNE

To make your own old-timey country song, use the lyrics included here, and combine them in any order you choose. Use a tune of your choice.

Sample lyrics

"Ah love _____" (choose one):

> you
>
> ma dawg
>
> beer

"Ah've lost _____" (choose one):

> ma love
>
> ma dawg
>
> ma mind

"Ah've found _____" (any of the above)

"You've broke _____" (choose one):

> ma heart
>
> ma truck
>
> ma arm

When going country, don't forget the hat!

Ted Seele

are many musical ensembles that use the kazoo with other instrumentation. Possible groups include jug and kitchen bands; hokum, skiffle, and shuffle bands; and country string bands. The instrumentation in each of these groups varies according to the group needs. Some commonly used instruments appropriate for use in combination with kazoos for these ensembles are the washtub bass, comb and tissue paper, finger cymbals, spoons, folk harp, banjo, and guitar.

Gospel Kazoo Groups

Gospel and church kazooing have been popular since the 19th century. For church outings, picnics, and bus trips, kazoos provide affordable accompaniment for hymns, motets, and other good-news and spiritual singing.

Hands-off fingering technique (see page 39) is particularly effective in gospel kazooing, since it leaves both hands free for rhythmic clapping and other percussive effects such as spoon playing or bones accompaniment.

Classical Kazooing: Maximizing the Minimal

Classical kazooing is the zenith,

SYMPHONIC KAZOOING

Leonard Bernstein, a man of rare insight and vision, brought symphonic kazooing to audiences on more than one occasion, but the kazoo has only begun to make inroads in the symphonic world.

The most successful symphonic kazooing has been accomplished by Kazoophony, in its program "Music vs. Noise." Performances with the Syracuse Symphony, Tulsa Philharmonic, Erie Youth Orchestra, and San Antonio Symphony have all been more successful than would seem possible.

"Eine Kleine Nachtmusik" by Mozart also transfers easily to kazoo in the Kazoophony arrangement entitled "I'm Inclined to Kazoomusik," by Wolfgang Amadeus Mozartsky. It uses the string quartet arrangement for four-part kazoo harmony, with a percussion part added to enhance the beat. For kazooists, the second or slow movement is generally omitted, since kazoo resonance does not lend itself well to extended lyrical passages. It tends to change the timbre to irritating tone color long before the notes end.

Bettman/Corbis

the crème de la crème of kazooing. With moments of experimentation and study, even the musically marginal can kazoo. However, the more accomplished the musician, the more masterful the results.

For the expert kazooist, it is imperative to give 150 percent for real mastery of this minimal instrument. Contrary to what you might imagine, the best classical kazooists are usually instrumental (wind or brass) musicians, not singers. While pitch is important, voice quality is democratically leveled by the equalizing resonator, so instrumental articulation is crucial and opera singers have no advantage. The world's best known classical kazooists are

in Kazoophony, which has a cast of thousands, only a few of whom are available for any given performance.

Lost Chord Kazooists:
Often, great classical kazooists are lost to the art due to lack of effort. For example, legendary pianist Glenn Gould might have been a great kazooist, if only he had applied himself. If you listen carefully to recordings, you will hear him instinctively humming along (vocally, without kazoo).

Classical practice exercise for the unitone kazooist: The following is a practice exercise for classical kazooing.

For this exercise (whether you have perfect pitch or don't care either way), you will need a pitch pipe or piano to give the starting pitch for each part.

The exercise is based on the "Beermeistersinger's Song" from *Tannheuser Busch* and can be mastered by kazooists of limited range and experience (one-note agility). Count the rests carefully, beating with your foot if necessary.

If you should happen upon an 80-piece orchestra and an

operatic cast with the rest of the musical score, this composition could be performed in its entirety. (Due to cultural arts budget restrictions, it was not possible to publish all of the orchestra parts here. This is the kazoo transcription of the fifth horn part only.)

CLASSICAL PRACTICE EXERCISE FOR UNITONE KAZOOIST

This is only an excerpt from the original, which is much longer, but most kazooists will have their hands (and their mouths) full with this much.

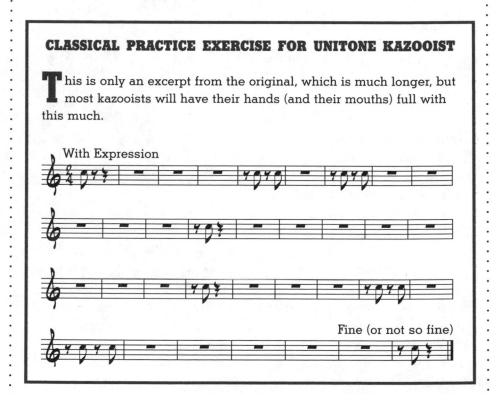

CHAPTER FIVE

EVERYDAY

(and Special-Occasion)

KAZOOING

Yoga Kazooing

Whether following Kazoo-daism as a way of life or just seeking exercise, yoga kazooing is a soothing pastime.

First putting down a dust mat, your goal is to breathe (inhale and exhale) while stretch-ing your body into positions for which it was never intended. Imitation of animal postures is popular, and repeated mantras such as "ohm-ohm-ohm" and other inspirationally pleasing animal sounds can be kazooed to accompany contortion.

Positions are as varied as the imagination and

The kazoo in the lotus

154

include "crouching kazooist, lurking in bushes to ambush audiences, like lion waiting for dinner"; "monkey vocalizing and showing off in tree"; "buzzing fly, facing upward with legs folded"; "barking bird dog pointing to ruffled grouse"; and so on. "Turtle sleeping," "flamingo seeking lawn position," and "butterfly flitting" are more difficult to articulate with audible sound, so the challenge is left to the individual kazooist. The most popular position among both professional union kazooists and amateurs alike is, however, rest position.

Troubleshooting usually falls into code red or code blue. If your face turns red like a tomato, give it a rest. You are trying too hard. If you turn blue, you are doing too many inhales and not enough exhales.

Après Ski Kazoo-Alongs and Kazoo-Skidoo Races

The usual yodeling and folk song kazoo-alongs are always good fun for lodge entertainment, provided everyone within earshot is amenable. Be advised that there is no safety issue with meltdown next to the fireplace under normal conditions, since the melting point for good-quality plastic kazoos will withstand the reflected heat, provided you don't try to toast them in the coals for warmth.

For those still needing to whet competitive urges, try Kazoo-Skidoo Races.[10] Attach two popsicle sticks to each kazoo, using Velcro or other adhesive substance to create your race vehicle. On a snowy slope (out of ski and snowmobile traffic areas), set up a start and finish line in the snow to conduct races. Award prizes according to whim— fastest, slowest, best-dressed, fanciest design, and so on.

[10]For Southern climates without convenient snow surface, Kazoo-Skidoo Races can also be accomplished on non-traffic-area paved surfaces or sloped tables by adding wheels to the kazoo barrel. This is not as difficult as it might seem, if you dismantle a suitably sized toy car and attach the wheel chassis to the kazoo.

X-treme Kazooing

X-treme Kazooing is the seemingly dangerous sport that combines the thrills of extreme creativity with the great satisfaction of kazoo playing. Instead of photographing your garden gnome traveling to exotic places, pack your kazoo and photograph your instrument, yourself, and/or your friends to compete for most creative extreme kazooing occurrence. (For those on limited budgets, you don't have to leave your computer to do this, since photo image enhancement can take you anywhere, if you have the skill.) Post your entry at www.X-tremeKazooing.com. All activities are undertaken at your own risk and must meet standards posted on the site.

Naval Maneuvers (Boating)

Clearly, all-weather kazoos and life jackets all around is the rule. As is common sense under any conditions, never spit or kazoo to windward.

For seagoing kazooists, there are infinite possibilities. Sea chanteys can be either chanted with words or hummed. Other perennial favorites with the naval crowd are hornpipes and ceremonial music such as "Anchors Away," "The Marines' Hymn," "Hail to the Chief Petty Officer," and John Philip Kazooza marches; gourmet galley music, such as "Truffles and Flourishes" and "Mess Call"; and boatswain's calls, such as "All Hands," "Belay," and "Heave Something."

Using kazoos as fishing lures is as yet untested for effectiveness, but if you attempt this, be sure to remove the resonating membrane before fishing and replace it before making music.

Pirating Music

For pirate buffs, there are innumerable raunchy songs, many of which involve rum, exaggerations, cursing, and bad grammar. There are also many guttural utterances such as "Arrr!" "Avast, mateys!" and "Shiver me timbers!" which meant much to pirates but make no sense to current generations. Thus it doesn't matter if anyone can understand your pirate articulations. If you wear the appropriate pirate costume, no one (other than parents or the authorities) is likely to question you. (For parrot noises, see page 68.)

High-Tech Kazooing

Cyber Cell Phone Bands

Truckers, commuters, and fellow travelers! Dolly Parton, Tim McGraw, Bette Midler, Garth Brooks, Paul McCartney, and everyone else! Bring amusement into your on-the-road time. Cyberband with other similarly inclined kazooists. While video-conferencing is always an option, it requires too much set-up time for most pickup groups. Put on your headset, ring up buddies on your cell phone, and kazoo together on the road.

CYBER PHONE BAND PRACTICE EXERCISE

"Kazoobee Doobie" (to the tune of "Peas, Peas, Eatin' Goober Peas")

Chorus
Doobie, doobie, doobie, doo
Doobie, doobie, doo.
Doobie, doobie, doobie, doo
Doobie, doobie, doo.
Playin' ma kazoo.
(Spoken: "Then I reached down and put on my cell phone head-set.")

Verse 1
Ridin' down the highway, playin'
    ma kazoo,
Wavin' to ma neighbors, howdy
    doody doo,

Talkin' on ma cell phone, yackety
    yackety yak,
Playin', wavin', talkin', coast to
    coast and back.

Chorus
(sing, then repeat on kazoo)
(Fade out kazooing medley of favorite tunes at end . . .)

Kazoo Google Grouping

Create your own kazooing Google group. On the Internet, go to http://groups.google.com. Click on "Create a group," and follow instructions to create your own private kazoo group or open it up to banding with the public. Get messages in your groups via e-mail or read them on the Web, with Google-protected security. Wear appropriate techiewear, as dictated by personal taste.

Flash Mob Events
Instigated by e-mail, this requires a mob of kazooists to suddenly assemble at a prearranged public location and act out a performance art task, according to some loosely constructed instructions. Kazooists should then melt into the crowd or background setting before apprehension by any authorities. Be sure and choose appropriate venues and tasks to avoid public annoyance charges. Public parks, wilderness areas, and private property with permission of the owners are all good choices.

Corporate Band Bonding
As with any other kazoo band, the key to corporate band

success is creative management and flexibility. Obviously, when more than one concert is involved, band membership will vary according to personnel movements within the company, such as hiring and firing. Normal attrition must also be taken into to account, including the demographic problems of transfers, maternity leave, and quitting for lack of proper incentives.

Since corporate bands have an economic unit (employment by the company) as their basis, the membership tends to be fairly stable. Often the same band persons show up year after year, particularly when kazoo and uniforms are supplied by the company. In this case, aging employees may require refresher

---

CELL PHONE RING TONES

Be the envy of all your fellow theatergoers and business-meeting attendees. To have your own resplendent kazoo ring tones, record your favorite tune and convert it into a WAV file for downloading onto a receptive cell phone. Otherwise, wait to download Kazoophony tones when they get around to offering their own unique kazootone selection online at www.kazoos.com.

To take full advantage of the marvelous capabilities of your distinctive kazootone rings, press playback to page yourself in order to be noticed. Also, in case of emergencies, use playback to extract yourself from unruly family gatherings, dating situations gone wrong, or other disasters requiring clever exit tactics.

> **Kazoo unto others, as you would have others kazoo unto you.**

training to make up for differences in the energetic marching techniques they so easily put into action in the past. Sympathetic personnel directors can facilitate graduation into golden age and senior citizen techniques, the use of motorized transportation in parades, and so on.

An exemplary example of corporate adaptability is the 39th Street Marching Band and Sis Boom Bah Chorus, which has moved and also aged gracefully since its original formation. It is now the Broadway Between 4th and Washington Place Sis Boom Bah Chorus and Golden Age Marching Band.

Loyalty can be demonstrated by corporate officers' financial support of their band and by active participation. At the Viking Electronic Company in Hudson, Wisconsin, for example, CEO Don Springer carried the banner in the Hot Air Affair Ballooning and Kazoo Parade. Kazoos were supplied and employees encouraged to use company time and their own ingenuity to modify their instruments.

Corporate Band Bonding Challenge Instructions:
Each team selects a celebrity management model from the list below and creates kazoo marketing strategies in that style. Competitors may use, but are not limited by, the suggested guidelines.

Donald Trump Management Style: Flamboyance and risktaking (particularly in hairstyle), inventive infighting, with special attention to termination skills. The signature phrase "You're fired" can be kazooed to a higher level, eliminating team members by using the enhanced-vocabulary "Termination Note (Wrap Song)."

Kazoo-speak in rhythm, with rhythmic accompaniment on office wastebaskets. Use appropriate Firing Squad choreography.

Even dogs can get in on the kazoo act.

David Strick/Redux

*"Termination Note
(Wrap Song)"*

You are declared excess
    and selectively impacted;
In other words—dejobbed,
    downsized, electively
    extracted—
Furthermore, dismissed,
    discharged, drummed
    out, displaced—
That means—dehired, dis-
    acquired, funeral-pyred,
    and literally erased . . .
And furthermore:

You are dumped out, kicked
    out, tossed out, and axed!
Given the boot, thrown on
    your ear—your walking
    papers faxed.
Ejected, rejected, deselected,
    and completely bounced . . .
You're out of here forever—
    officially renounced!
That's right . . .
Take a powder, you're history—
    get out of the kitchen heat . . .
You're demeritus, emeritus—
    most completely obsolete!

You're on the shelf, no use
    yourself—you're positively
    warehouse-ted . . . (pause)
Officially expelled,
    expunged—and now for-
    ever ousted. . . . ! ! ! !
What goes around comes
    around . . . dontcha know—
You are terminated, extermi-
    nated—presence not
    required,
Position eliminated—
    involuntarily retired . . .
Hasta la vista, baby—
    Farewell, it's time to go . . .
So long, take your leave—

(Singing)
Wha-ha-ta-hey, hoya-ta-ho,
    hoya-ta-ho!
'Course, it's . . . nothing
    personal.

*(Kazoo the music for "Taps"
to end the team firing squad
activity.)*

*Oprah Winfrey–Style
Teambuilding Exercise:*
It's all about spirit and self,
relationships, generosity,
bonding, counseling, and
audience wish fulfillment.
As a team, design a corporate
giveaway that will benefit,
rather than bankrupt, your
company. Think need, not
greed.

*Martha Stewart Management
Style:* Market manipulation,
high-style kazoos for low-end
users, along with decorative cur-
tains, designer kazoos, party
favor-tism, and domestic kazooing touches. Make sure you
apply the Martha Stewart "look"
to add special value to ordinary
situations.

*Bill Gates Technological
Teambuilding:* Attention to
design detail, takeovers, and market control should be included

in your Kazoogate strategy. Technological advances and product improvements such as kazoo-shape mousepads, mouse covers, decorated monitors, etc., may be incorporated into your plan.

Stephen Jobs Apple Strategy: Imagine you are the Johnny Appleseed of kazooing. Invent new hot-look products, simplify techniques, and unify your eclectic colleagues as you electrify the market.

Combat Kazooing

For those who revel in the bombardment of pitches and enjoy fearless engagement with the audience, here are the latest techniques for Combat Kazooing.

Stealth Kazooing

For beginners who prefer to perfect their art in secret before

going public—try stealth kazooing. This technique is also recommended for undercover kazooing in dangerous territory.

At an undisclosed location or isolated outpost (out of enemy earshot), practice on a camouflaged kazoo to remain undiscovered, until you reach the desired level of expertise.

If you do not possess a Harry Potter invisibility cloak, be sure to choose the appropriate camouflage for your covert cover. For example, do not employ forest

COMBAT KAZOO REPORT

In 2004, Kazoobie Company provided the 173rd Army Airborne with custom Kombat Kazoos. The idea (initiated by 173rd Airborne's webmaster Jim Brady) was to use kazoos as a unique communication device, like the clickers (cricket noise-makers) paratroopers employed to identify each other in the dark during the World War II Normandy Invasion. Reports on the communications value of combat kazooing in Iraq appear inconclusive, but the entertainment value is priceless.

green camouflage when kazooing where desert sand pattern is appropriate.

Urban Stealth Kazooing
In city areas, blend yourself and your instrument into the background with camouflage appropriate to the urban environment.

Vehicle-Assisted Bombardment
(Driveby Kazooing)

In addition to fashion coordination, stealth kazooists should provide for proper driveby transportation. Armored Hummer trucks (Humvees) are especially recommended, since the vehicles not only shield from enemy attack but also contribute motorized hummer harmony.

Quality Time Kazooing
Play Together to Stay Together

Kazoo banding is an activity in which age doesn't matter, skill is admired but not required, and any number can participate.

Children, like adults, love the freedom to experiment with sound, but also like to be part of something that is fun and familiar. Simple tunes, camp songs, American and ethnic songs, animal sounds, or just plain noise can all be enjoyed, within reasonable boundaries and at the right time. If it is not reasonable or

Let our people blow.

the right time, either hand out earplugs or collect the instruments and redistribute them when it is. (See deactivating the instrument, page 41.)

When to Begin Kazooing

It is believed by some that we are all born with the innate ability to kazoo. If it is left uncultivated, we lose the ability sometime around puberty. Thus, many adults require refresher courses. Children are naturals, but for safety reasons, children under the age of three should not be allowed to kazoo unless carefully supervised.[11]

[11]Common sense tells any responsible adult that children under the age of three shouldn't do much of anything unsupervised, so this should not create any particular hardship.

Prenatal and Early Childhood Kazooing

Children's fascination with sound is present at birth, and probably begins in utero. Certainly some subtle kazooing by the parents during pregnancy can do no harm, provided the volume level and musical selections are appropriate for in utero infant consumption. (See page 50 for muting techniques.)

EVENTS OF NOTE

Celebrity kazoo band leaders Rick Hubbard (Rick Hubbard's All-Kid Kazoo Band), "Weird Al" Yankovich, trumpeter Al Hirt, and the Crown Prince of Bavaria have all led the world's largest Kazoo Band and Chicken dances, an annual Oktoberfest event in September in Cincinnati, Ohio. Everyone is welcome.

After birth, you should postpone formal lessons until infants are old enough to be persuaded to trade in their pacifier (mouth plug or binkie) for an instrument. Security blankets, softies, and other attached or handheld artifacts are no barrier to success, since even the smallest kazooist can master one-handed or no-handed kazooing. However, they are never too young to begin listening appreciation.

"Do-It-Yourself" Neighborhood Parades

Kazooists love a parade, so celebrate every occasion with organized or free-form banding. Here is the perfect activity for no budget, low skills, and high enthusiasm. A few kazoos, homemade decorations, neighbors, bicycles, and a drum roll—and you're on your way.

Emergency Preparedness

Rather than throwing money and blame at problems after a disaster, be prepared. Do that ahead of time.

Disaster Preparedness Kit

- Label children's and other household members' kazoos so they can identify one another in case of separation. Use glow-in-the dark paint for names and attach flashing LEDs (light-emitting diodes) to avoid collisions.[12]
- Peanut butter and crackers
- Water to quench thirst after peanut butter and crackers
- Hand-cranked amplifiers to project kazoo music at high

volume over vast, disaster-stricken areas. (Nothing bucks up dampened spirits or inspires entertaining debate quite like enthusiastic renditions of amplified kazoo music.)

[12] Obviously, children must be taught at the earliest possible age to keep their kazoos with them at all times.

Emergency Preparedness Simulation Drill

To simulate disaster situation:

1. Bar the exits so nobody in the captive audience gets away without permission.

2. For a long enough period to make household occupants crazy, turn off power, water, and all utilities (no phones, cell phones, computers, TVs, radios, CDs, video games, or other electronic devices).

3. Do what people used to do without modern conveniences (legal behavior only, please).

Party Kazooing

Impromptu Kazoo Groups

Impromptu kazoo groups spring up everywhere, at parties, rallies, and conventions, wherever people gather for fun. Longevity of the group is generally dependent on the length of the event or the arrival of law enforcement officials to require compliance with local noise ordinances.

Wedding Bands

For cost-effective versatility, it is only necessary to learn one tune to accompany all wedding needs. Lohengrin Kaminsky's popular

HERE GOES THE BRIDE

Andante Moderato ♩=100   Lohengrin Kaminsky

Tai yoop tah tee; Tai yoop tah tee;

Tai yoop tah tee tumm tah tum tee tah tee.

"Here Goes the Bride" can serve as the march-in, then works for the reception with varied rhythms (tango, waltz, rock, hip-hop, and so on). For those getting married a second time, just play everything twice.

"Here Goes the Bride"
Tai yoop tah tee;
Tai yoop tah tee;
Tai yoop tah tee

Tumm
Tah tum
Tee tah tee.

Divorce Divergence

Remember that you will need to hold two parties, since participants now prefer to be apart, rather than sharing expenses.

"Here Goes the Bride" also works for divorce music, by

inverting the order (playing it backward). For ceremonial alert to the guests (and for safety considerations), be sure to use the backing truck reversal warning sound prior to playing (see page 84).

Decorations:
In the kazooist's tradition of keeping it simple, decorate and

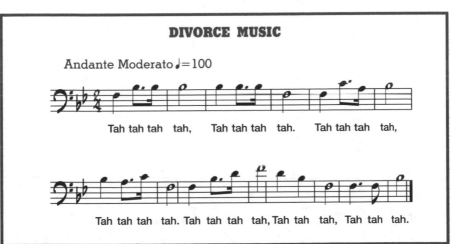

> **You can't eat your cake and kazoo at the same time.**

color coordinate everything in white for weddings, black for divorce. For the wedding cake, use traditional bride and groom figures on the top layer. For divorce cakes, separate the bride and groom figurines and place the appropriate partner head-first in the frosting. (Be sure to get the right one to honor the remaining party at that party.)

Birthday Party Serenade

Place a paper "blowout" in the smaller end of a kazoo and tape it to hold it in place. Kazoo the first verse of "Happy Birthday to You," using articulation, as follows:

Verse #1 (kazooed)
Doo-dee doo-doo doo doo;
Dee doo-doo-doo doo doo.
Doo dee doo-doo dee doo doo;
Dee Doo Doo Doo Doo?

AVOIDING THE BIRTHDAY SONG COPYRIGHT

Although music is an integral part of birthday celebration, the rights to the traditional six-note "Happy Birthday" song are protected by copyright. This explains why commercial outfits do elaborate arrangements of something or other else to celebrate, although home users are allowed to kazoo whatever they want.

If you wish to spice up your commercial performance with a new unprotected version, here are some words in Dutch for any tune you feel like. (You won't need the correct pronunciation, since kazooing will obscure articulation anyway.)

DUTCH TREAT HAPPY BIRTHDAY

Lang zal ze leven lang zal
  ze leven lang zal ze leven
  in de gloria in de gloria
  in de gloria hiep hiep
  hoera!

In translation, it is "May you live in Gloria," which seems positive, although we're not precisely sure of the exact meaning.

*Verse #2 (sung; adapt tune
  to accommodate lyrics)*
Happy birthday to you;
I'm kazooing to you.
I wish you a happy birthday;
What more can I say?

Birthday Balloon Party Favors
Suspend kazoos from helium-filled party balloons, allowing missile to float to the ceiling for decoration. If you do this outdoors, anchor the balloons

to something earthbound before releasing them in decorative floating formations.

All-Purpose Holiday Caroling

Kazoophony's arrangement of "Ludakravian Jingles Bells" is the most popular all-purpose holiday carol; it takes care of Christmas, Hanukkah, and Kwanzaa at the same time. Choreography includes "air balalaika" (Russian version of strumming air guitar) and a grand finale of Cossack squat dancing while seated on chairs.

New Year's Eve Traditional

Place paper "blowout" mechanism in the smaller end of a kazoo and tape it securely in place. Sing updated words to "Auld Lang Syne," thereby eliminating any need to remember the original, archaic lyrics. Kazoo the chorus. When finished kazooing for the evening, carefully remove paper "blowout" and store in a cool, dry place for use at birthday occasions or for next New Year's.

NATIONAL KAZOO DAY

National Kazoo Day occurs annually (although in some regions, more often) on or about January 28—or whenever convenient for the kazooist. As stated by founder Chaplain Willard Rahn of the Joyful Noise Kazoo Band at the Homewood Retirement Home in Williamsport, Maryland, "After all, we have to be flexible." Many kazooists choose the fourth Thursday in January because it's handy.

Verse:
Should auld acquaintance
be forgot
And never brought to mind?
I've lost him (her) once
again, I fear
Maybe I'll find him (her)
here next year.

Chorus:[13]
Dah dah-dah dah-dah dah
bah dah
Dah dah-dah dah-bah dah

[13]"For Auld Lange Syne, my dear," etc.,
are the normal lyrics here.

Bah dah bah dah bah dah
bah dah
Dah-dah dah-bah dah-dah
dah

Super Bowl Sunday Homefront Party

To engage at-home participation in festive activity,
provide each Super Bowl
party guest with a kazoo for
entertainment and a football
helmet for protection, in case of
differences of opinion. Every

partygoer will then be musically equipped, endlessly entertained, and properly protected to enjoy all the ups, while those on the field experience the downs.

Being Crafty with Kazoos: Home and Gardening Projects

In the great craft tradition of going to enormous effort and expense to make something useless out of something that was perfectly functional to begin with, kazoos can be put to many uses around the home, banquet hall, and garden.

Kazoo Birdhouses

After building a splendidly decorated birdhouse, add a decorative kazoo perch that will allow performance of birdcalls, in order to attract tenants.

Instrument Case

With hours of painstaking effort, extraordinary small-motor skills, fabric, zippers, scissors, and velvet lining material, you, too, can take pride in packaging your instrument. A chic instrument carrying case is suitable for both concert and everyday use.

Until now only two have been made (due to the eight-hour effort involved), both made by my mom—one for me and one for Famous Amos (Wally), who asked my mom nicely (and also sent her cookies in an autographed tin).

Garden Borderlines

Kazoo arrangements can also be integrated into your garden plan, as borders for your walkway or garden outlines. Be sure and use durable plastic varieties, since gold plate or metal models will not hold up well outdoors.

Flower Holders

Flower arrangements are a snap using kazoos as colorful vials to hold flowers upright. Kazoos are available in a wide range of hues, in solids, bicolor, and multicolors, to coordinate with your color scheme.

Planting Artistic Ideas

By sticking kazoos in potting soil, with a certain amount of botanical skill, you can coax plants to grow up through all-weather (plastic) kazoo barrels to form interesting planters. Some horticulturists recommend taking tropical plants into the shower to create the correct rain-forest atmosphere. However, for kazooists this may be counterproductive, since the purpose of taking a shower is to get rid of dirt, not bring in extra with you.

Wind Chimes

Strands of kazoos suspended by weatherproof twine can be decoratively dangled to form wind chimes for the garden or home. In fact, neighbors may find this gentle tinkling less annoying than standard kazooing.

Kirigami Kazooing

While origami is the art of paper folding, Kirigami Kazooing is even more challenging because it requires folding *and* cutting.

> *Materials*
> Paper
> Scissors
> Pencil

> *Step 1*
> Fold paper along dotted lines to make accordion pleats.

Step 2
Draw a kazoo outline on the folded paper.

Step 3
Cut around the outline (not the ends at the folds), keeping paper folded.

Tod Seelie

Step 4
No, no! Do NOT cut through the fold! Go back to Step 1.

Step 5
Unfold the paper. You now have a Kirigami Kazoo chain. Decorate the halls, home, office, or yourself.

Kazoo Makeovers

Paint, fabrics, glue, etc. should meet approved U.S. Consumer Safety Standards, as should any accessories added. (See the small parts and sharp edges sections of government safety standards.) Wallpapering is somewhat difficult to master, but decoupage is always an option.

Adding a Kazoo Room to Your House

While the most obvious makeover possibilities are for the instruments themselves, if you do not already have a kazoo utility room or practice space, you can greatly increase the value of your home by adding one. It may be as elaborate as your energy, imagination, and budget dictate. Recording facilities, performance monitors, and soundproofing can tremendously enhance any solo or group efforts; craft work-benches, storage for art supplies and materials, and instrument display cases for accessories and collectibles are a must.

Joyful Noise Festive Holiday Wreaths

Kazoo the holidays your way, crafting a playable wreath for a circle of friends. Kazoos of Christmas Past or Present (antique or contemporary) can be made into holiday ornaments, as well as woven into tasteful wreaths.

The advantage of circular kazoo wreathing is that you can create a multifunctional work of art that you can either play or display. Be sure to arrange kazoo mouthpieces to face toward the outside of the wreath, so you and a group of friends have easy access for ensemble playing.

Branching Out into Kazoo Trees

Ornamentation for celebratory trees is not limited to any particular season—it can be expanded for decorative effects for any occasion. Be sure to use all-weather instruments for outdoor decorating, employing fitted shower caps to protect the delicate resonating membranes (and any celebratory kazooists gathered round) from inclement weather.

Outdoor Holiday Kazooing

For outdoor celebrations, be sure to use instruments adapted to the climate. Northern climes

require all-weather (plastic)
to prevent frostbite or tongue
adhesion to the instrument,
especially in winter. For tropical
kazooing, use appropriate sun
protection for the kazooist (sun-
screen) and the kazoo (protective
umbrella).

FOUL-WEATHER RECORD

On Jan. 1, 1978, temperatures
were low and spirits high
as Rochester, New York, first
claimed the record for most
foul-weather kazooists in the
streets (outdoors), with 34,000
intrepid participants at a New
Year's Eve celebration, led by
Rochester Philharmonic
Assistant Conductor Isaiah
Jackson. Yearly competition
for this record (if any) varies
according to interest and
temperatures nationwide.

Other Fa-la-la Projects
(Marzipan or Cookie Dough Kazoos)

Although these are musically
nonfunctional, they have other
useful attributes. They can be
consumed as snacks during
rehearsal or performance. They
can also be preserved with lacquer spray for decorative but
no-longer-edible purposes such
as Christmas tree ornaments,
table decorations, and art objects
(often referred to as "objets d'art,"
so they seem more important).

What to Do with New Year's "Day After" Kazoos

There are some who reserve
kazooing for New Year's
Eve. To avoid loss or theft
between New Year's Eves, proper
interim storage is an important

consideration. Lavalieres (neck-lace attachments) keep kazoos close at hand but are lumpy to sleep on. If stored in drawers or pockets, always clear the barrel of lint or debris when reactivating.

One Final Note

You have now been thoroughly immersed in the history and background of your instrument and are versed in its technique. You are ready to go forth and kazoo with pride. However, before you go, a word of caution:

Although kazoo playing is not fattening, nor is it injurious to your health, it is only fair to warn you that it may be habit-forming. . . .

APPENDIX

Historic Kazoos

When Is a Kazoo Not a Kazoo?

If it talks like a kazoo, sounds like a kazoo, but doesn't look like a kazoo, it probably isn't. Play it, enjoy it, but recognize that it may be a kazoo cousin, not a true kazoo.[14]

[14]According to liner notes on the Ringo Starr album *Ringo,* the song "You're Sixteen" featured Paul McCartney playing "mouth saxe." It is actually a kazoo, which he plays with vocal rather than instrumental technique. He chose to name it something else, because kazooists can pretty much do what they want and McCartney is no exception.

Walt Disney Mickey Mouse Kazoo®

Amusing miniature Mickey Mouse figure with megaphone. All-plastic construction, with wide circular mouthpiece is especially well suited to the facial structure of the preschooler. (Quaker Oats Company)

Hi-Fi or Amplifier Kazoo

This was also known in the 1940s as a "Kazoophone." An

enlarged horn-shape bell attached to the turret markedly amplifies the volume and channels the sound. (Kazoo Company, Inc.)

Hum-A-Zoo

The Hum-a-Zoo is a close relative of, but not identical to, the standard kazoo. It was first patented in 1923 and is still manufactured by Trophy Music, Inc., of Cleveland, Ohio.

Clarinet Kazoo

A 10½-inch metal instrument, with gold finish and red plastic safety mouthpiece. Perforated finger holes serve only as decoration. (Kazoo Company, Inc.)

Bugle Kazoo

A foot-long, heavyweight metal bugle. It has a gold finish, with red plastic safety mouthpiece and red decorative tassel. A bugle-shape resonating chamber produces sound suitable for wake-up duty or military alert. (Kazoo Company, Inc.)

Slide Trombone Kazoo

A metal kazoo, with gold lacquer finish and red plastic safety mouthpiece. It has a movable slide that extends size from 11 inches to 13½, but does not musically affect the instrument. (Kazoobie, Inc.)

Cornet Kazoo

A metal kazoo with useless red plastic keys that press down and spring back. It has a gold finish, with red plastic safety mouthpiece. (Kazoo Company, Inc.)

Hum's the word

Kazoophony, the World's Largest Quartet

Described by *The Wall Street Journal* as "America's Premier Kazoo Group," Kazoophony brings professional kazooing to its very zenith.[15] Spawned in the shadow of the Eastman School of Music in Rochester, New York, the group was founded to encourage the art of kazoo playing and promote musical enrichment all over the world.

[15] Glowing descriptions of Kazoophony are barely influenced at all by the author's lifetime involvement as leader and kazoo-keeper for the group.

The remarkable and widely ignored Kazoophony is a unique musical group that spoofs the formality and ritual surrounding music, while taking its kazooing seriously. It enthusiastically assaults all forms of music, including classical, rock, country, jazz, opera, blues, marching band, or anything else in its path.

"Until I saw this group [Kazoophony], I thought I'd heard everything."
Composer Aaron Copland

John Stanton

Kazoophony has appeared extensively on radio and television *(Tonight Show, Prairie Home Companion),* at Lincoln Center and Town Hall, with symphony orchestras, at colleges and festivals . . . and at the opening of the new Yellow Trucking Center on the site of the Emerson Street Dump in Rochester, New York. It has also been banned twice in Britain and reviewed by *Playboy,* all without doing anything rude that its members knew about.

Kazoophony originally performed as the 80-piece Ludakravian Philharmonica until the budget cut, when it was reduced to the world's largest (five member) kazoo quartet. (The usual number for a kazoo quartet is seven, so Kazoophony is still missing two people.) Kazoophonists are currently in rest position, awaiting any sign of demand for performance.

Kazoodaphiles

For those who wish to admire as well as play the kazoo, there are opportunities for fans and groupies. The leader of

WORLD UNIFICATION CAMPAIGN

First America, then the world! Broaden your range and band together internationally. Kazooing knows no boundaries and voices can be raised world-wide in no languages whatsoever. The Dutch, the English, and the Canadians are already kazooing their part—the Finns, the Chinese, the Japanese, and the Russians are all making themselves heard. Kazoodaphiles unite!

the Kazoophony Fan Club is Kazooperman, a dedicated kazoo aficionado who lives in San Francisco. Fans who wish to join the club may do so on-line at www.howtokazoo.com.

Campaign to Make the Kazoo the National Instrument

America has a national bird, a national song, . . . and a national debt. It may not need those, either, so why not make the kazoo the national instrument? "Tippecanoe and play your kazoo." "Two kazoos in every garage." . . .

The kazoo is a natural choice for the American national instrument, since it is one of a very small number of instruments native to America. An exhaustive search reveals that in addition to

the kazoo, the other authentic American instruments are the sousaphone (named after John Philip Sousa), the glass harmonica (invented by Benjamin Franklin), and the Iroquois water drum (invented by the Iroquois). The kazoo clearly should be the front-runner in this group.

David Perlman

HOORAY FOR THE RED-WHITE-AND-BLUE KAZOO!

It is time for a sitting Congress to step forward together and stand firmly behind the kazoo nationalization issue. But don't call me, contact your senator or congressperson (see page 195).

ARGUMENTS FOR KAZOO NATIONALIZATION:

1. It's an American invention.
2. Kazoos are always colorful, without being color-dependent.
3. Kazoos are affordable for all and a great leveler, giving everyone an equal chance to maximize the minimal.
4. The kazoo is the instrument of the common people. After all, it's nothing if not common.
5. No kazooist is left behind, unless he or she makes a wrong turn and loses the band.
6. This most egalitarian of instruments allows equal-opportunity kazooing for everyone, regardless of musical ability, political allegiance, ethnic choice, gender, species, or other special interests. The unitone or arbitrary pitch kazooist is every bit as welcome as the musical maestro, making up in enthusiasm what he/she may lack in musicianship.
7. Membership requirements for spontaneous groups are nonexclusive, generally dependent on the number of armed kazooists rounded up.
8. One nation of kazooists, taking liberties, has few consequences for all!

For some time, an attempt has been made to make the kazoo the American national instrument. Every American president since President Nixon and President Carter has either turned down or ignored requests for assistance. It is possible that no one remembered to approach either of the Presidents Bush, but President Clinton definitely did not respond. Rochester, New York, and New York City have passed resolutions in favor of the kazoo, and more places might follow suit if they think of it.

The kazoo nationalization issue has also been endorsed by such luminaries as Paul Newman. Newman was quick to say that although he appreciates culture, he would not be attending any kazoo concerts because they conflict with his regular bowling night.

The campaign on behalf of the kazoo continues, and it is now at a stage described by onlookers as "dormant." This may be due to the economy and the politically amorphous attitudes of dedicated kazooists, who wander off and practice rather than campaign.

To assist the Kazoo Campaign, complete and send the petition (facing page) to elected officials to express your view. To find your senator or representative, the President or First Lady, ask a librarian or see www.senate.gov, www.house.gov, or www.whitehouse.gov. Address the petition accordingly:

Dear Senator _____,
Dear Representative _____,
Dear Mr. President, or
Dear First Lady _____.

To: The Honorable _____

Address: _____

Date: _____

Re: KAZOO AS NATIONAL INSTRUMENT

Dear_____

Please join Barbara Stewart and Kazoophony in the Campaign to Make the Kazoo the National Instrument to Keep America Humming!

We already have a national song, a national bird, and a national debt. We may not need those either, but why not make the kazoo the national instrument? This is the one nonpartisan issue on which both red and blue states can agree, since it truly matters to no one. The kazoo is clearly the ultimate democratic instrument. While only a small elite can play the sousaphone, any constituent of yours who can talk, sing, or hum can kazoo.

According to jazz legend, this uniquely American instrument was invented in Macon, Georgia, in the 1840s by an American black named Alabama Vest and made to his specifications by a German-American clockmaker named Thaddeus Von Clegg. It is a real instrument not a toy, and there is still one major manufacturer in the United States (Kazoobie Company), which has at least three or more employees.

Widely associated with the 4th of July, New Year's, and other American celebrations, never has the "Star-Spangled Banner" sounded so daunting as when performed on kazoos. Nothing else quite captures the individual character and "do it yourself" spirit like the kazoo. Even though kazooists have been victimized by high oil prices that raised the cost of plastic kazoos by 70 percent, the bands play on.

We ask you to step forward and stand up in the sitting Congress to raise your voice in support of the kazoo as national instrument.

Thank you for your attention to this important matter. I would appreciate a prompt response from you.

Sincerely,

(PRINT YOUR NAME)_____

(SIGNATURE)_____

(ADDRESS)_____

_____